"An invaluable resource for grandparents who want to better understand and support their transgender grandchildren. Through heartfelt letters and stories, alongside well researched information, this book provides insight, support, and practical tips for grandparents as they strive to learn how to best demonstrate their love and support for their transgender grandchildren. Any grandparent who wants to learn how to be a positive and loving presence in their transgender grandchild's life needs to read this book."

—Liz Dyer, Founder of Real Mama Bears

"A must-read if you are a grandparent, parent, or a person who wants to learn how to love, support, and celebrate transgender, gender-diverse, and gender-creative young people."

—Diane Ehrensaft, PhD, Director of Mental Health, UCSF Benioff Children's Hospital Child and Adolescent Gender Center

"*A Grand Love* is a gem that gently shares critical information, offers heartfelt personal stories, and models what unconditional love can look like!"

—D. M. Maynard, author of *The Reflective Workbook for Parents and Families of Transgender and Non-Binary Children*

"A groundbreaking masterpiece of profound enlightenment, illuminating the path for grandparents to wholeheartedly embrace their transgender and non-binary grandchildren. Overflowing with an abundance of knowledge, thought-provoking reflections, and heartfelt personal stories and interviews, Barkin's work not only educates but also will deeply resonate with readers, empowering them with the tools and wisdom needed to navigate the complexities of understanding and acceptance."

—Jeanette Jennings, mother of Jazz Jennings

"A profoundly moving and enlightening read, this book invites us into the intimate and often unspoken journeys of grandparents navigating the complex path of understanding, acceptance, and love for their transgender grandchildren. Through a collection of heartfelt stories, it not only sheds light on the unique challenges faced by these families but also illuminates the boundless capacity for love and acceptance that can transcend generations. Each narrative serves as a beacon of hope and a guide for anyone looking to support their loved ones with empathy and grace. Whether you are directly impacted or an ally seeking deeper insight, *A Grand Love* offers a powerful testament to the enduring strength of familial bonds in the face of societal norms and expectations. A must-read for anyone on their own journey towards acceptance and integration

—Jeff B⟨ ⟩h,
I Just ⟨ ⟩er

T0190640

by the same author

He's Always Been My Son
A Mother's Story about Raising Her Transgender Son
Janna Barkin
ISBN 978 1 78592 747 8
eISBN 978 1 78450 525 7

of related interest

My Child Told Me They're Trans...What Do I Do?
A Q&A Guide for Parents of Trans Children
Brynn Tannehill
ISBN 978 1 83997 277 5
eISBN 978 1 83997 278 2

**Everything You Ever Wanted to Know about
Trans (But Were Afraid to Ask)**
Brynn Tannehill
ISBN 978 1 78592 826 0
eISBN 978 1 78450 956 9

Growing Older as a Trans and/or Non-Binary Person
A Support Guide
Jennie Kermode
ISBN 978 1 78775 363 1
eISBN 978 1 78775 364 8

A GRAND LOVE

Stories for Grandparents of Transgender Grandchildren

JANNA BARKIN

Jessica Kingsley Publishers
London and Philadelphia

First published in Great Britain in 2024 by Jessica Kingsley Publishers
An imprint of John Murray Press

1

Copyright © Janna Barkin 2024

The right of Janna Barkin to be identified as the Author
of the Work has been asserted by her in accordance with
the Copyright, Designs and Patents Act 1988.

Foreword copyright © Amaya Barkin 2024

Content warning: This book contains mentions of transphobia and suicide.

A CIP catalogue record for this title is available from
the British Library and the Library of Congress

ISBN 978 1 83997 764 0
eISBN 978 1 83997 765 7

Printed and bound in the United States by Integrated Books International

Jessica Kingsley Publishers' policy is to use papers that are natural,
renewable and recyclable products and made from wood grown in
sustainable forests. The logging and manufacturing processes are expected
to conform to the environmental regulations of the country of origin.

Jessica Kingsley Publishers
Carmelite House
50 Victoria Embankment
London EC4Y 0DZ

www.jkp.com

John Murray Press
Part of Hodder & Stoughton Limited
An Hachette UK Company

*This book is dedicated to my Grandma Essie and Grampa Joe, who were **always** there for me. We lived together in a multigenerational house, and they were active caregivers to my brothers and me. Their love was a comfort and a blessing, as are the memories I have of them in my life.*

Contents

Foreword

AMAYA BARKIN

My family as a whole has been very accepting of my transition. I like to think that my grandparents were particularly easy adapters to my new pronouns and gender identity. Even so, I'm sure it was challenging for them to some extent.

Because I always gravitated to clothing from the boys'/men's section even as a young child, the clothing I wore more or less remained the same when I transitioned. So did the short haircut I have maintained since kindergarten through today. My outward appearance remained much the same, but my pronouns did change. Still, the frequency of pronoun-related mistakes made by my grandparents when talking about me was no more than I would expect from anyone trying to undo 16 years of habit.

Despite their reception and acceptance of my identity while in my presence, I wonder what my grandparents thought, felt, or even said when I was not around? Were they confused? Was it a surprise? Did they question my ability to make the decision to transition at such a young age? Were there any opposing opinions that surfaced for them when I decided to get top surgery or start testosterone?

I'm sure they had questions. Who or what did they turn to in order to answer these questions?

In many ways, I'm grateful I did not have to be the recipient of this line of questioning. Perhaps my grandparents shielded me from such questions to avoid giving me the wrong impression of their mindset. They never made me feel as though I was less deserving of the love they had always given me.

Many gender-diverse people do not have this luxury. Others are publicly scrutinized and shamed by their grandparents.

I have never shied away from answering questions from people who would like more education on the topic of gender. I would have welcomed the opportunity at any time to connect with any of my grandparents in such a way. Sadly, three of my four grandparents are no longer alive. I wish I'd had more occasions with my grandparents, or with anyone else, to discuss how I view myself and how I wish others to view me. Though I am grateful for the lack of inquisition from people in general, I have always felt equally grateful to talk about such things if and when there has been any inquiry.

I am sure there are many people who want to educate themselves without scrutiny, without embarrassment for themselves or their transgender or gender-diverse family members, and without receiving judgment for not being up to date. In an ideal world, grandparents would always feel safe and secure asking questions of their grandchildren to learn more about their identity and would do so with an open mind. Maybe my own grandparents, and others like them, did not feel prepared, or felt they were not armed with the right language to have this kind of discussion.

Grandparents who do not want to give their grandchildren the wrong impression, or who may have other concerns about approaching their grandchildren about this topic, may be more comfortable seeking outside expertise and talking to peers with similar experiences. Literature such as the book you are about to read can provide a "safe space" for grandparents who want more knowledge and preparation tools to help them understand and accept their gender-diverse grandchildren for who they are.

Introduction

Dear Grandparent,

It is my deepest wish that the stories herein—stories of challenges and struggles, of curiosity and courage, of acceptance and love—will support, inform, and inspire you on your own journey.

Loving our grandchildren for exactly who they are is truly *A Grand Love*.

There was not a single *aha!* moment when I knew my own child was transgender. My husband and I were keenly aware that our child was not your average tomboy (if there is such a thing). One might say the signs were there, from the clothing he chose to wear, to the so-called "boy toys" he consistently chose for his play, to the way he carried himself and moved his body. Of course, such signs don't always mean someone is transgender. (Do toys or colors really have a gender?) Looking back, my husband Gabriel and I can see that our child was always showing us who he was. It just took us a while to understand and to recognize him for who he really is.

Before we go on, an important note about pronouns and gender-specific words. To be clear, I will use male pronouns for Amaya consistently throughout this book, even though our family and community used female pronouns for Amaya until he asked us to switch at age 14. Likewise, I will use the appropriate male, female, or gender-neutral pronouns for all other people in this book, with respect to each individual's gender identity. Also, readers should note that I may use gender-neutral words (*they*, *them*, and *their*) instead of gender-specific words (*he/she*, *her/him*, or *her/his*) when I refer to individuals.

My understanding and acceptance of my son developed over a long period of time and tracked closely with his own emergent understanding and self-acceptance regarding his gender identity. When I first started looking for information and support to help me understand my child, I was lucky to find some great resources. But, at that time, there were scant few voices and websites providing useful information and perspectives for those of us parenting a transgender child. Now, there are many great resources available on the internet and elsewhere. Sadly, there is also a lot of misinformation—and a lot of fear, hate, and ignorance.

In my work today as a facilitator of parent support groups, a workshop presenter, and a parent coach, I strive to provide a safe and informational environment for parents, grandparents, family members, friends, educators, and audiences at corporations and non-profit organizations to learn more about what it is like to be the parent of, and advocate for, a transgender child of any age. Above all, I aim to emphasize the importance of loving them for exactly who they are.

My first book, *He's Always Been My Son: A Mother's Story about Raising Her Transgender Son* was a #1 bestseller on Amazon and continues to be a valuable resource for parents, family members, and others.[1] It has always been my hope that telling my story about raising our transgender child, and sharing what I have learned along the way, will foster more compassion, understanding, and acceptance in our society.

A Grand Love: Stories for Grandparents of Transgender Grandchildren is a continuation of that intention. The book you are reading was born from the many inspiring interactions I have had with grandparents of transgender people.

In 2020, during the long and isolating Covid-19 pandemic,

I founded an online support group for grandparents of transgender grandchildren and I continue to lead this group today. Originally based (virtually speaking) at The Spahr Center in Corte Madera, California,[2] we have had participants in attendance from all over the United States. One participant, "Grandma E from Iowa," describes our group as such:

"We grandparents are a blanket of love covering all LGBTQ+ grandchildren across the nation."

Transgender people have never been more visible in the modern era than they are right now. There is significant evidence that transgender and gender-diverse people are most successful when they have the support, love, and acceptance of their parents and families.[3] Some of the stories in this book are positive affirmations of family support, particularly from grandparents. Sadly, many people do not have the benefit of love and acceptance from some or all of their family members, and I have included a few stories intended to serve as cautionary tales, and to provide encouragement for us all to do better.

Grandparents can play a crucial role in family dynamics. Their love, understanding, and acceptance is critical.

Grandparents who become aware they have a grandchild whose gender identity doesn't match the gender they were assigned at birth can feel confused and alone. In our rapidly changing world (so it may seem), there may be generational differences that make it even more challenging for grandparents to accept their transgender grandchildren. Likewise, they may not know, or be able to find, generational peers who are experiencing something similar.

Despite a growing body of knowledge in many professional fields, there are numerous therapists, counsellors, teachers, and school administrators who do not have the skills needed to support transgender or gender-expansive children, nor their parents and grandparents. There are many social, educational, and even (in some regions) legal challenges that make it difficult for some families to find therapeutic and educational support.

Enter *A Grand Love: Stories for Grandparents of Transgender Grandchildren.*

This book provides uplifting, educational guidance through stories told from my perspective as both a mother of an adult trans child and a coach and advocate for families of gender-diverse people; by grandparents of transgender grandchildren; and by transgender people themselves. *A Grand Love* also provides resources, including information on the latest research on gender, lists of non-profits and other organizations supporting transgender youth and families, and a selection of online and local support groups.

My son Amaya, who is now 25 (he transitioned when he was 15), once said to me, "Mom, you think about gender way more than I do." This makes me very happy because it was not always true. There was a time in his early teens when his gender was all he could think of. It was all he could do just to get through another day, struggling with what we eventually learned was gender dysphoria. Today, he is happy, healthy, and living as his authentic self. He thinks of gender very little, which underscores how successful he has been in resolving his dysphoria and living as his authentic self. I, on the other hand, think of gender often because I have made it my life's work to educate and support people regarding gender.

Every child deserves to be loved and supported unconditionally. Being transgender is just one more beautiful, normal variation of being human.

Our family is so grateful to everyone in our extended family, to our friends, and to our greater community, who have accepted and embraced our son's transition. We know we are fortunate in this regard, as many trans people do not have the support Amaya has. I am here to advocate, inspire, educate, and, most importantly, save lives. I am glad you are here too.

Janna's Top 5 Tips for Grandparents of Transgender Grandchildren

From the moment our grandchildren are born, we develop an image of who our grandchildren will turn out to be. We may even daydream about our future grandchildren—right down to their names, their gender, the things they will do, the adventures they will have, and even the hand-me-downs they will wear.

As life unfolds, some of these expectations may come to fruition. More often than not, however, we must adjust to what *is*. There are many variations of being human that will veer from our preconceived images of who our grandchildren will be, and those variations will undoubtedly challenge our original notions and expectations. We therefore may need to adjust our expectations of who *we* are in relation to our grandchildren. As grandparents, we will likely be asked to adjust and adapt in many ways. Some of these adjustments are easier to make than others.

Let's be clear: **Being transgender is not a "lifestyle choice."**

As I said earlier, being transgender is just one more beautiful, normal variation of being human. Unfortunately, like many human variations, being transgender is not without challenges. Those challenges all too often include gender dysphoria, which can lead to tragic outcomes for those who do not receive care and find resolution. (I will define "gender dysphoria," and many other terms, in the glossary section of this book.) Having the support of family is the number one way to prevent those tragic outcomes, including depression and suicide, among transgender people.[1]

Every child deserves to be loved and supported unconditionally. Grandparents are an essential component of that support.

With this in mind, here are my top five tips for grandparents of transgender grandchildren:

1. **Be Love.** Love your grandchild. All children deserve to be loved unconditionally. (Yes, this bears repeating.) It is a sure sign your grandchild trusts you if they tell you something deeply personal, such as when they invite you into their experience by telling you, "I'm trans."

2. **Be Approachable.** Regardless of your grandchild's gender identity, remind them that you are there for them. You might say, "You can tell me anything. You can text me, send me an email. You can draw a picture. You can talk to me in whatever way works for you. And you don't have to do any of that, and still, I am here." Respond in a way that keeps the door open.

3. **Be Patient.** Have patience with your grandchild—and with yourself. Your grandchild is probably many steps ahead of you. They probably have been thinking about this for much longer than you know. It's okay for you to take time to process this new information and learn more about it.

4. **Be Curious.** Keep an open mind. It's okay to not know the answers. You can ask your grandchild, "Can you tell me more about that?" Or ask them, "How do you feel about that?" Sometimes they don't want to be asked. That's okay too. If you sense (or if they tell you) that's the case, find someone you *can* ask.

5. **Be Supported.** Seek out knowledgeable, gender-informed, affirming support. There are numerous online support groups for family members of transgender people, including some groups specifically for grandparents. You might even find there is an in-person support group in your area. Ask a trusted friend to help you find resources. Find a good therapist or a mentor to help you tread this new path. There is a wealth of information available online and elsewhere to help you along.

I encourage you to keep the list above handy as you explore the offerings in this book. Ask yourself, "How can I be present and supportive to my grandchild—and myself—in this stage of our journey?"

Just as each transgender person is unique, each family member is also unique. Each of you will have your own journey on the path toward understanding, acceptance, and integration. The stories contained in this book are examples of that journey, *A Grand Love*. I offer them as a guide to help you on your own unique path.

Reflections: A Letter to My Beloved

LINDA MASIA, AMAYA'S MATERNAL GRANDMOTHER

(Excerpt from *He's Always Been My Son*)

Dear Aaron,

I have a very interesting story to tell you. Of course, I've already told you, but now I will write it down.

When you suddenly and sadly left us in 1997, Janna was seven months pregnant. We had suffered Dad's loss (Janna's grandfather) just two years prior, not so sudden but also so sad. After you died, Janna stayed with me for about a month. She needed to leave and go back home to California to have her baby, but also she needed to be with me and Mom, her dear Gramma. Since Janna had planned another home birth, she did not know if a boy or girl would be arriving, but she decided with Gabe that this baby, if a son, would be named Aaron Joseph in memory and honor of you and Dad. If a girl, she would be named for both of you, but using just the A and J initials.

A little over three months go by and Janna delivers—a girl! She is named Amaya Jael. Emily, your first and only grandchild (whom you loved beyond loving), loves "her baby," and life goes on. Emily was such a girly girl, loving the skirts and tights, fancy socks and hair stuff, and angel wings. Amaya, at an early age, perhaps two-ish, began to show a preference for coveralls, jeans, trucks, nothing with ruffles or bright colors, no skirts or tights, no angel wings. A couple of years go by and we are thinking, wow, Amaya is surely a real tomboy, not liking anything feminine, not clothes or toys or activities. The family would come to New York to visit, and I'd see Emily choosing to wear the same kind of outfit Janna was wearing, but Amaya would check to see what Gabe was wearing and dressed like her dad.

2001 arrives and brother Shawn is getting married. Shawn and Val invite Emily and Amaya to be flower girls. Oh, wonderful for Emily, pretty dress and shoes and a flower basket. Not so much for Amaya, who also did wear a pretty dress and shoes and carry a flower basket but did not at all wear a smile. Of course, we can look back now and understand, but at the time, we did not "get it." Incidentally, Mom would call Amaya "he," and I would say, "Mom, Amaya is a girl!"

As it will, time goes by, and I see Janna, Gabe, and the kids a couple of times a year, once here on the East Coast and once there on the West Coast. I see Amaya growing taller and developing a feminine body, but insisting on a short, boy haircut, and boy sneakers, and boy clothes purchased in the boys' department. I see a kind of moody kid, yet sweet and loving, plays sports, does well in school. But joyous, no. I hear and see Emily pushing Amaya in the back to encourage her sibling to "stand up straight" and I don't understand why Amaya won't stand up straight myself.

Perhaps it just took a really long time to find the words, but Amaya thankfully did, and told his truth: "I am a boy!" Janna tells Emily that he wants to be called her brother, not her sister. Emily is fine with that and so the journey begins. So many people, upon meeting Amaya, already thought he was a boy, never thought they were meeting a girl.

Amaya is 16, physical changes continue, and he looks more and more like a boy. I notice that when we eat out, he is always drumming on the table. The family comes east for a visit, and as usual I invite the East Coast family to dinner to see the West Coasters. Everyone here now knows that Amaya is transgender. The nieces and nephews, aunts, uncles, and cousins are here. Everything is normal, everything is fine and warm. We are all respectful of pronouns, Amaya doesn't mind if there is an occasional slip, we are all learning. What a great family we have. No doubts, only acceptance.

The youngest cousin, perhaps he is three, puts both hands on Amaya's face and says "Amaya, I just love you!"

Amaya is 18. I attended his high school graduation. He earned several honors and a small scholarship and will start college in the fall. He is tall, handsome, funny, fun, and smart. He has his dad's gift of sarcasm, his mom's gift of kindness, and, hopefully, his Grampa Aaron's gifts of patience and unwavering, unconditional love.

Love,
Linda

In 2023, Linda added a P.S. for this book:

Dear Aaron,

Amaya is 25! Time for an update. It seems very strange to write that number, time goes by so quickly, doesn't it. He had a very successful four years of college, graduating *summa cum laude*. He learned much, made friends (many of them will become lifelong friends, I'm sure), and chose to stay in Portland as he enters the real world.

Amaya and his partner, Chayla, have now been together for several years. They are happy, productive, and hard-working, with good dreams for the future. And they've added a dog to their family. His name is Freddie, and they really love him.

I had the pleasure of a visit from Amaya not so very long ago. It was wonderful to see him, and to see him sleeping in the same bed he slept in oh so many years ago. I am so very proud of the man Amaya has grown to be. The adjective "gentleman" really fits him, especially when you break it into the two words. He is a kind, gentle, and loving man, and has many of your qualities. I love him and know you would too.

My love,
Linda

Finally, in 2023, Linda offers these words of wisdom for grandparents new to the journey:

"Our family is much further along than you all are. You will see, in time, that you will get used to all of this, and it won't be hard any more. Over the years, it will just become who that person is."

What Does That Mean?
A Glossary for This Book

The words we use to describe others and ourselves are important. Words we use to describe ourselves tell the world who we are and how we want to be seen. Words we use to describe others tell them what we think about who they are. Those descriptions are based most often on what we have discerned from their own words and behavior, as well as information from other inputs including peers, cultural norms, political/religious views, environmental factors, and more.

Here are some words I use to describe myself:

- I am a mom.
- I am a woman.
- I am cisgender.

These are words I might use to describe my youngest child:

- He is my son.
- He is a man.
- He is transgender.

Some of these words may be familiar to you, and some may be new. There has been a shift (some say it's a revolution) in the way people think about and talk about gender. The language of gender is always evolving, and it can be hard to keep up. That's okay. Humans are wonderfully capable of learning new things and adapting. And, once again, I am here to help.

Given that words are vital for understanding someone's gender identity, it is important that I define some of the key terms used in this book. This is by no means a complete list, and some of the words in this glossary may have different meanings to different people. Just like there is no one way to be a human being, there is no one way to be transgender.

For a more in-depth exploration of terms and definitions, there is a plethora of resources available online (including the website I used as primary references for this glossary, hosted by Gender Spectrum).[1,2,3]

Let's be clear: *Gender and sexual orientation are different things.*

Our sexual orientation and our gender are separate, though related, parts of our overall identity.

- *Gender* is personal and refers to how we each see ourselves.
- *Sexual orientation*, or *sexual identity*, is interpersonal, and refers to which people we are physically, emotionally, and/ or romantically attracted to.

Gender is multidimensional. Gender is not only based on physiological traits, rather, it is a combination of physiological, psychological, and social factors. It is not necessarily determined by biological sex traits. More on this in a moment.

Sexual orientation, often referred to as sexual identity, is a way to describe whom someone is attracted to. Here are some terms that describe sexual orientation:

- *Heterosexual* (attracted to the opposite gender)
- *Homosexual* (attracted to the same gender)
- *Bisexual* (attracted to one's own and at least one other gender)
- *Pansexual* (attracted to all or any gender)
- *Asexual* (largely not attracted to anyone, and/or largely not interested in sex)

Gender identity is different from *sexual orientation*, although they are interrelated. Gender is about "who you are," and sexual orientation is about "who you are attracted to." The words people use to describe *sexual orientation* have to do with:

- an individual's own gender identity
- the gender identity of the person they are attracted to; and
- the words that they feel best describe the relationship between them.

Developmentally, a child typically has a core sense of *gender* at a younger age than the age at which they become aware of their *sexual orientation* (or sexuality in general).

This book focuses mainly on gender: what it means to be transgender and the experience of having a transgender grandchild. Let's take a deeper dive into the concept of gender.

WHAT IS GENDER?
Gender has three components:

1. Body
The biological component of gender
This is what we typically mean when we use the term "sex" to describe the gender of a newborn baby. This component refers to the body a person is born with and includes body parts such

as genitalia, DNA, chromosomes, hormones, brain functions, etc. (In the U.S., the U.K., and pretty much everywhere else, the gender marked on a birth certificate is based on the genitalia visible at birth.)

2. Expression
The social component of gender
The way one presents to the outer world, and how the outer world perceives and treats someone with regard to gender. This includes choices in clothes, style, hair, activities, and communication style. This component also includes the assumptions people make about these choices based on stereotypes with regard to gender.

3. Identity
The psychological component of gender
A person's deeply felt inner sense of self as masculine, feminine, a blend of both, or neither, or something else. Gender identity can correspond to *or* differ from the sex assigned at birth.

Understanding the differences between these three gender components may be a new conceptualization for people who are used to thinking of gender as something that is determined solely by the body parts someone is born with.

The definition of *gender* above provides a general framework for understanding the rest of the terms in this glossary.

GENDER-RELATED TERMS

- **Sex:** This refers to the label, *male* or *female*, noted at the time of birth based on visible genitalia. Also sometimes known as birth sex, natal sex, bio-sex, or sex assigned at birth.

- **Gender spectrum:** A construct that describes gender as a continuum with male characteristics toward one end and female characteristics toward the other. Many gender identities exist on the spectrum between the two ends, or exist outside the spectrum, or are not at all aligned with the spectrum.
- **Gender binary:** A construct that recognizes only two distinct categories, *male* and *female*. Both *cisgender* and *transgender* people (these terms are defined below) can have a gender identity that fits into the binary construct. However, not all gender identities exist within the binary framework.
- **Cisgender:** This term is used to identify people whose gender identity and sex assigned at birth are congruent. To simplify, this describes people who feel inside that their gender matches their sex assigned at birth and marked on their birth certificate.
- **Transgender:** As currently used, the word *transgender* is an umbrella term used broadly to encompass anyone whose gender identity does not align with the sex assigned to them at birth. (This term used to refer more specifically to someone whose gender identity is the opposite of their sex assigned at birth.) People may identify as transgender whether or not they have had, or plan to have, any medical interventions. (Examples of medical interventions include a variety of gender-affirmation surgeries and hormonal treatments.) To be clear, not all transgender people have, or are able to access, medical interventions and treatments. A person who has had any or all of these interventions may not identify as transgender.
- **Trans:** An abbreviation for *transgender*. These two words are sometimes used interchangeably. In addition, *trans* is used by some people as a catchall phrase to include all people whose gender identity and/or gender expression does not align with the gender marked on their birth certificate.

- **Assigned male at birth (AMAB):** An individual who was born with "boy" parts and assumed to be male at birth.
- **Assigned female at birth (AFAB):** An individual who was born with "girl" parts and assumed to be female at birth.
- **MTF:** Abbreviation of "male to female." A term that describes someone who was assigned male gender at birth but whose gender identity is female.
- **FTM:** Abbreviation of "female to male." A term that describes someone who was assigned female gender at birth but whose gender identity is male.
- **Non-binary:** An umbrella term used for gender identities that are not exclusively male or female (see *gender binary* above). People who identify as *non-binary* may feel both male and female, or neither, or someplace in-between, or some combination of all of these.
- **Gender fluid:** A non-binary gender identity that describes a person who experiences their gender identity as fluid, in that it flows or shifts rather than being set or static.
- **Agender:** A non-binary gender identity that describes a person who is without gender, or who feels no connection to any gender. Someone who feels neither male nor female, and/or who does not want to be seen as either by others may describe themselves as *agender*.
- **Pangender:** A non-binary gender identity that describes a person who has a feeling of an expansive gender experience that may include any combination of binary identities such as male, female, and/or non-binary. Some people who identify as *pangender* may have gender identities that go beyond the current knowledge and terminology regarding gender.
- **Intersex:** Someone who is born with chromosomes, hormones, genitalia, and/or other physical sex characteristics that are not distinctly male or female. About 1 percent of children are born with sex characteristics that do not fit

typical binary expectations of male. Most *intersex* people are not at risk medically. Typically, *intersex* babies will have a male or female sex assigned at birth by their doctors/family based on their predominant characteristics or because the intersex characteristics are not observed at that time. Many parents these days choose not to assign a gender to a child born with *intersex* characteristics, allowing their child to be self-determining with regard to their gender identity.

- **Gender expansive or gender creative:** These broad terms are used often to describe someone who may not fit into typical male/female stereotypes of behavior or expression in one or more ways. These individuals often challenge the expectations around gender within their community. Other similar terms include *gender non-conforming* and *gender diverse*.

- **Genderqueer:** A broad term used to describe people whose gender identity does not fit into conventional gender norms.

  The word *queer* was historically, and is still used today, as a political statement. People who do not fit into the gender binary construct have long been the brunt of derogatory insults (and worse). The word *queer*, when used in reference to gender identity and sexual orientation, initially evolved as a slur directed at LGBTQ people.

  Today, identifying as queer, or *genderqueer,* can be a way for people who do not comport to dominant societal gender norms to identify with the struggle for acceptance and equality. Rather than shrinking from the use of *queer*, many people have chosen instead to take ownership of the word. Thus, in recent years, the word *Queer*, with a capital "Q," has evolved into a catch-all descriptor adopted by many people who want to identify themselves as part of the broad LGBTQ+ community.

- **Gender questioning:** Someone who is questioning or exploring their gender identity.

- **Gender diverse:** People with diverse (non-cis) gender identities, and/or people who express gender in a way that could be considered "out of the box" by societal norms and standards.
- **Transboy:** A child who was assigned a female sex at birth and identifies as a boy.
- **Transgirl:** A child who was assigned a male sex at birth and identifies as a girl.
- **Transsexual:** An outdated term that refers specifically to a person who has had sex reassignment surgery and transitioned to the sex opposite of the one they were assigned at birth. While some people still use *transsexual* to describe themselves, most trans people today prefer the word *transgender*.

   Note that, as mentioned before, not all transgender people have surgery, and surgery is not what makes someone transgender. Using the word *transgender* therefore allows a person to maintain privacy in that regard.
- **Cross dresser:** Someone who enjoys dressing in clothing stereotypically worn by the opposite sex. People who are *cross dressers* may or may not be transgender.
- **Gender congruence:** The feeling of harmony with regard to one's gender. *Gender congruence* is when a person's identity, body, and expression align. This looks different for everyone, and the process of finding congruence is unique to each individual.
- **Gender dysphoria:** This is both a clinical term (with an uppercase "G" and "D"), and also an inner feeling (with a lowercase "g" and "d"). The latter is defined as a profound, persistent state of unhappiness, unease, and/or dissatisfaction that may occur when a person's internal sense of who they are does not align with the sex they were assigned at birth. A person can experience varying degrees of *gender dysphoria* that range from uncomfortable to deeply distressing. Often,

gender dysphoria can be relieved as a person experiences increasing levels of gender congruence (via, for example, maturity and self-acceptance, social/peer/family acceptance, or therapy and/or medical interventions).

Gender Dysphoria is also a clinical term found in the American Psychiatric Association's Diagnostic and Statistical Manual of Mental Disorders.[4] In 2013, this diagnosis replaced a previous entry, "Gender Identity Disorder," which was classified as a psychological disorder. However, being transgender or gender non-conforming is no longer considered a mental disorder. Therefore, the diagnosis has been replaced by Gender Dysphoria, which refers to the psychological distress that results from an incongruence between one's sex assigned at birth and one's gender identity.[5] If someone experiences Gender Dysphoria, it can be helpful to work with a skilled mental health professional. Not all transgender people report suffering from gender dysphoria; this doesn't make them any less transgender.

- **Transition:** The process a person goes through to align aspects of their life to be consistent with their gender identity. Transition broadly encompasses the many changes a person makes in order to affirm and live consistently with their gender identity. Transition can be described as finding gender congruence. Transition can happen on several different levels including:
  - Social transition: Changes to social identifiers may include new or augmented pronouns, name, clothing, hairstyle, and many other outward-facing expressions which can be observed in a person's day-to-day life and their interactions with others.
  - Legal transition: Individuals may seek to change government-issued documents such as birth certificates, driver's licenses, and passports in order to have their legal status align with their gender identity.

- *Medical transition*: An individual may use medicines such as hormone blockers or cross-sex hormones to align their physical characteristics with their gender identification.
- *Surgical transition*: Some people choose to modify their body surgically via addition or removal of gender-associated physical traits. This can include (but is not limited to) the alteration of genitalia, facial reconstruction, and/or laser hair removal.

- **Gender-affirming surgery (this is also known as gender-confirmation surgery):** Often abbreviated as GAS or GCS, this term refers to specific surgical procedures, or more broadly, to all such procedures, in which an individual's genitalia is altered to be congruent with their gender identity.
- **Bottom surgery:** This is a term used to describe GAS procedures that alter genitalia.
- **Top surgery:** This is a term used to describe GAS procedures that include removal of the breasts and creation of a male chest, or the addition of breast implants and creation of a female chest. Non-binary people may also choose *top surgery* to align their body with their inner sense of gender.
- **Pronouns:** Relative to gender, *pronouns* are how we refer to others in the third person to reflect their gender identity—for instance, as *they/them*, *she/her*, *he/him*. Some people use a combination of *pronouns* such as *she/they*.
- **Dead name:** The name a transgender person was given at birth, or a nickname given at any point in their life, which that person no longer uses or identifies with following a transition. It is not appropriate to use someone's *dead name* in their presence or in any other circumstance, even if they are not present, unless they have said it is okay to do so.
- **Misgender:** To *misgender* someone is to use pronouns, adjectives, or a dead name (or any other name) corre-

sponding to the wrong gender. *Misgendering* may be an accident or a purposeful act. While a person who misgenders someone may not mean any harm, misgendering can feel very hurtful to the person of lived experience.

There are also many terms that are broadly considered outdated, offensive, or otherwise no longer acceptable when talking about gender today. Here are some words that are no longer used, except as noted below:

- *Gender Identity Disorder* (an outdated and no longer relevant diagnosis)
- *Tranny*
- *Transvestite*

A note about the words *tranny, transvestite,* and *transsexual*: these terms are sometimes used by people in the trans community to describe themselves, either broadly or perhaps just within a specific circle of their lives. Some people in the trans community have told me that their use of these terms to describe themselves is a way to reclaim words that have historically been used as slurs against them.

There are also some terms that some people continue to use even though other people consider them outdated. Included in this category are some of the acronyms you'll find in the glossary above, including *FTM, MTF, AMAB,* and *AFAB*. While these acronyms can be accurate in their description for some individuals, many trans people do not like these terms. They feel they are dismissive and inappropriate. Such terms, they say, label a person as *not this* but as *that*, so to speak, or *not that then* but *this now* (e.g., "I *was* male, but *now* I am female"). Many trans people say they have always been who they are, regardless of what labels they were given at birth—and therefore, to use a term such as *male to female* or *assigned male at birth* is not accurate and can feel demeaning, "othering," or just plain wrong. As I mentioned earlier, what words one uses to describe oneself is a choice for each individual and not something for other people to decide.

So now, let's go back to those words I used to describe myself above:

- I am a mom.
- I am a woman.
- I am cisgender.

Regarding that last one, saying I am *cisgender* means that in my core, I know myself to be a woman (that's my gender identity), which aligns with the determination made at my birth and placed on my birth certificate that I was female because I was born with a vagina (the sex assigned at birth). My gender identity and sex assigned at birth are congruent, and I identify as female. I was born this way.

Here are the words I used above to describe my youngest child:

- He is my son.
- He is a man.
- He is transgender.

As defined above, *transgender* means one's gender identity does not align with the sex they were assigned when they were born. My child was born with female genitalia, so my child was assigned female. (That's his sex assigned at birth.) My son, in his core, knows himself to be male. (That's his gender identity.) He identifies first and foremost as male, and he is also transgender. He was born that way.

Part 1

FACT OR FAD?

Transgender. Non-binary. Gender fluid. Bi-gender. Agender. Pangender. Gender expansive.

These are just some of the words people use today to describe their gender identity. Facebook, until recently, had 54 gender markers one could choose from. Facebook continues to offer a wide variety of choices to identify one's gender, and even added a "custom" choice that allows users to enter anything they want.[1]

Increasing numbers of youth today question their gender, and there is a corresponding increase in the number of ways people choose to describe and name their gender. A recent UCLA study found that over a quarter of Californian kids aged 12 to 17 say they are viewed by others at school as gender non-conforming.[2] Alarmingly, the study also found that youth who identify as gender non-conforming and/or androgynous report higher levels of psychological distress than their gender-conforming peers. What's going on here?

Some people may wonder if this is a cultural fad that will eventually fade. Experts in the field say otherwise. In fact, our culture today is making great leaps and bounds regarding our understanding of gender identity. The latest research shows that gender is not a binary "black or white" paradigm constructed along rigid male or female lines.[3,4] Rather, gender includes a spectrum of identities ranging from male to female along several strata, and some identities even extend outside the spectrum itself. One's identity can exist anywhere within—or even outside of—this spectrum. A key to understanding gender identity conceptually is to recognize that it is defined foremost as a person's innermost sense of who they are with regard to gender. As with everything else about individuals, there are infinite variations to gender.

Dr Stephanie King, a licensed psychologist who specializes in working with youth and gender, told me:

> Today's youth are navigating a complex world. Each generation inherits the challenges of their predecessors while also simultaneously grappling with new issues of their own time. Some would argue that the current generation faces more challenges than any before them, while others believe this sentiment is common to every era.
>
> However, in recent years there has been an unprecedented focus on deconstructing and redefining gender—although many are familiar with the diverse interpretations of gender across cultures, the topic has never been as prominently discussed and, at times, brutally ridiculed as it is now.
>
> We are in the midst of a profound shift regarding identity, especially gender identity. The journey of self-understanding is complex and often evolves throughout one's life, encompassing various stages of growth. Understanding gender identity and expression is integral to this journey and cannot be left out, as it contributes to our capacity to evolve, reflect, and ultimately understand and love ourselves.

As visibility of transgender people has increased in our society, we see that many people have become familiar with what it means to be transgender. Understanding and acceptance are on upward trends in the U.S. (particularly in some regions), even in the face of the current political climate in our country. Even today, however, transgender people who transition and present clearly as either male or female have a higher likelihood of being accepted by their family and community compared to gender fluid and other non-binary identities. Gender-questioning or gender-expansive people do not fit into the binary male/female paradigm, and these people typically have a much more difficult time being understood, supported, and accepted.

Does it even matter if any of the aspects of gender identity are fad or fact? The results of a 2012 survey of transgender youth conducted by Ontario's Trans PULSE Project[5] revealed that trans youth feel the number one factor impacting their happiness and self-acceptance is parental support. Sadly, the survey results also show that, to the contrary, trans and gender-expansive youth without family support are in the highest risk pool for depression, anxiety, and suicide.

These are sobering statistics. Children who do not express gender in stereotypical ways *need* parents—and grandparents!—who are knowledgeable, flexible, and patient regarding gender identity and expression.

It is often surprising or shocking to grandparents when they discover their grandchild is not behaving in accordance with typical gender norms. Grandparents may feel anxiety or loss when they learn their grandchild is transgender. Those feelings may be compounded for grandparents whose grandchild defines themselves not merely as transgender, but as gender expansive, gender fluid, non-binary, agender, or anything else that does not fall cleanly into "male" or "female" buckets. There are people who describe themselves as "gender fluid"—meaning that they may feel they are male at certain times or in certain situations, but then later (in a minute, an hour, a day), or in a different environment, they feel as though a switch has flipped and they are female. Some people describe themselves as both male and female. Or as neither. In any case, the way someone expresses themself on the outside may not even match the way they feel or identify on the inside. The variety is seemingly endless, and grandparents are rarely well-equipped to understand it all.

It is often said that the *T* (for *transgender*) in *LGBT* is about 30 years behind the *L, G, and B* (for *lesbian, gay*, and *bisexual*) in terms of acceptance. As recently as three decades ago, parents and grandparents were far more likely than today to be distraught if their child/grandchild came out as gay. Currently, however, there is a much wider level of acceptance in the U.S. for gay or lesbian people *vis-à-vis* transgender people. Research by the Pew Research Center[6] shows that acceptance of lesbian, gay, bisexual, or transgender people increases with familiarity. For instance, the greater number of gay men a person knows, the more likely that person will be accepting of gay men in their community.

When we consider that up until very recently, more people reported knowing someone personally who is gay than they did someone who is transgender, it illustrates why there has been a corresponding lag in acceptance of transgender people. As acceptance of gays and lesbians has outpaced acceptance of gender-diverse people over the past few decades, grandparents who have learned they have a transgender grandchild have occasionally reported saying things to their children like, "Transgender? If only you were gay, it would be so much easier to understand and accept."

More recent data from a 2021 Pew Research Center survey[7] found that a growing number of people (42% of adults surveyed) say they know someone personally who is transgender and/or someone who uses gender-neutral pronouns. That is a big shift from a 2016 report,[8] in which only 10 percent of respondents said they knew someone who is transgender. And yet, even with this shift in visibility, Pew reports that comfort levels using gender-neutral pronouns have not changed.

By nature, humans are creatures who fear the unknown. But the frontier of what constitutes "the unknown" is ever-shifting. People in the U.S. today are becoming more familiar with, and increasingly more accepting of, transgender people who "cross over" from one gender to another. In popular culture, for instance, many people know of trans celebrities such as Jazz Jennings, Elliot Page, Caitlyn Jenner, and Laverne Cox, all of whom contribute to growing awareness and acceptance of transgender people. So naturally, as the "unknown" frontier shifts and transgender people increasingly become part of the "known," we find grandparents expressing fears along different boundaries: "Non-binary? If only you would choose a side. If you're trans fine, then just be a boy or a girl, but this in-between is just too much!"

Our society is making significant strides in understanding gender and gender identity, as well as how we relate to one another concerning gender. Gender is not confined to a simple binary categorization of "male" or "female," but instead exists along a diverse spectrum. As previously mentioned, this spectrum encompasses a wide range of possibilities, extending beyond traditional notions and including identities that transcend conventional boundaries.

To illustrate this dynamic, consider the "Gender & Sexuality Abacus" pictured below. Individuals can use a visual tool like this to describe their identity relative to gender and sexuality. As you read in the glossary in the last chapter, gender identity and sexuality are two different (albeit interrelated) things. *Gender identity* is personal, *sexuality* or *sexual identity* is interpersonal.

For some people, their gender identity, expression, and body have characteristics that are male, female, both, neither, or any unique combination of genders—and these characteristics may be fixed or fluid. Hence, for any given person, the "beads" of their Gender & Sexuality Abacus may not be placed all on one side or the other. Likewise, sexual preferences do not always fall neatly along either/or lines. Using a Gender & Sexuality Abacus as a visual tool to define oneself along multiple spectra (however limited and imperfect this depiction may be) allows for introspective insight and gives people an alternative way to express the subtle nuances and variations that shape us all.

Gender & Sexuality Abacus

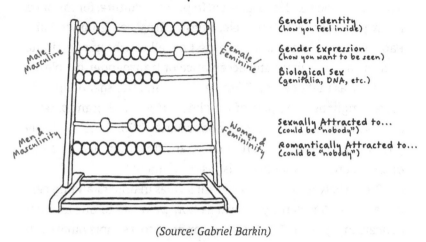

Gender Identity
(how you feel inside)

Gender Expression
(how you want to be seen)

Biological Sex
(genitalia, DNA, etc.)

Sexually Attracted to...
(could be "nobody")

Romantically Attracted to...
(could be "nobody")

Male/
Masculine

Female/
Feminine

Men &
Masculinity

Women &
Femininity

(Source: Gabriel Barkin)

Patience and acceptance grow out of understanding. Ari Sifuentes, LMFT, Therapist and Director of Mental Health at The Spahr Center in Corte Madera, California, offers this:

In recent years, we've witnessed a notable rise in the number of youth courageously stepping forward to embrace and share their true selves. This surge is not a passing trend but an unveiling of identities that have long existed, yet often remained hidden due to societal pressures and prejudices. It's essential to understand that this self-discovery is a profound journey, and creating a safe, supportive space for transgender youth is not just benevolent—it's imperative. Recognizing and affirming their identities allows these young individuals to flourish mentally, emotionally, and socially.

In the same breath, we must also address the diverse spectrum of gender identities. Non-binary identities stand as genuine and valid as any other, and while some may mistakenly perceive them as a phase or an "in-between" they are, in fact, deep-rooted expressions of self, deserving of equal respect and understanding.

Lastly, we cannot speak about gender diversity without highlighting that the support of peers and family plays a pivotal role in the well-being of transgender youth. These connections serve as protective buffers against the challenges they face, offering love, acceptance, and a sense of belonging. As advocates, therapists, friends, and families, our job is to fortify these bonds and ensure that every transgender young person feels seen, heard, and cherished.

Indeed, it can be very stressful, painful, and isolating to live a life that is neither authentic nor true to one's inner sense of self—and doing so can have devastating consequences. According to The Trevor Project's 2022 *Survey of LGBTQ Youth*, transgender and non-binary youth are at great risk of depression, anxiety, suicide, and self-harm, and these issues are reported at disproportionally high levels among transgender and gender non-conforming people. In fact, as many as 52 percent of transgender youth reported they had seriously considered suicide, a number almost double that of the general population. Transgender people who report the highest rates of success and happiness in their lives are those who say they were able to transition and live as their authentic selves with the support of their families and communities.[9]

It's time to shift our way of thinking.

Best practices evolve. Today's youth are finding new ways to describe their inner sense of gender, and they are also exploring ways of expressing that inner sense to the outer world. Is this just a fad? Or are the youth pushing us toward the future, a future in which all forms of gender identity and expression will be seen as valid and true?

Best Practices Evolve

LISA TREADWAY

I've been an early childhood educator in San Francisco for almost three decades. Throughout that time, I've had the privilege, pleasure, and responsibility of taking care of two-, three-, and four-year-olds in a loving, progressive, and supportive environment. The teachers and administrators at our school focus deeply on all aspects of a child's development. We believe that strong, positive relationships, where everyone feels respected and included, are the keys to a successful learning community. The messages and values we consciously impart to our youngest community members include acceptance of ourselves and others, the celebration of differences, critical and divergent thinking, conflict resolution, and physical and emotional safety. We celebrate each other's strengths and support each other's challenges and journeys. My fellow teachers and I strive to continually grow as educators— which, of course, means that over the years we have evolved in our thinking. What was a best practice *then* is not always a best practice *now*.

This is perhaps especially true in regard to our thinking about gender. Back in the late 1980s, a child named Andrew came to school each day thrilled to adorn himself with every sparkly necklace in the dress-up corner, and sometimes even the pink ballet tutu. We, the teachers, instinctively knew in our hearts that his right to do so should be supported wholeheartedly. It obviously brought Andrew such joy to gaze at himself and his adornments in the mirror! We reassured his dad that just because Andrew chose to play this way, it did not necessarily mean he might one day be gay. When other children inevitably commented with concern that Andrew was dressing like a girl, we knew how to respond to them: "It's not what you wear that makes you a boy or a girl, it's your *body* that makes you a boy or a girl." We gave the same message to the children who claimed that teacher Tim had "girl's hair" (because he wore it in a ponytail), and to those who teased Sarah for always playing with boys: "It's not how you look, what you do, or who you play with that make you a boy or a girl, it's your body. If you have a penis, you're a boy. If you have a vagina, you're a girl." We also thought it important to help children understand what we called *gender constancy*—"You were born a girl, so you will always be a girl. Girls grow up to be women, boys grow up to be men."

How our thinking has changed! At our school, we now understand that it's not, in fact, your body that makes you a boy or a girl. Gender is not binary, nor is it necessarily constant. We realize that one's biological gender is sometimes different from one's gender identity, and that neither is necessarily tied to gender presentation.

But how do we explain all of this to very young children, especially when their parents don't agree with our perspective? My colleagues and I struggle with this question. We have to do what we know is right for the children in our care while at the same time respecting the beliefs and values of our students' parents. Although attitudes have clearly shifted in general in our culture, we have not yet reached a point where all parents are comfortable with their three-year-old son wearing nail polish, or with their four-year-old daughter asking to wear boys' *Star Wars* underwear, or saying she wants to marry her best girlfriend. In partnership with parents, we do our best to listen, to acknowledge feelings, and to advocate without judgment for what we understand is best for the child. We explore and share current research. We explain to children that sometimes adults have different ideas. At the same time, we do not compromise those fundamental values that we and our school hold dear, especially when doing so might negatively impact a child's self-image and self-esteem.

So what words do we use currently in the classroom when children ask questions or make comments about gender? "It's not how you look, or what you do, or who you play with that makes you a boy or a girl. Sometimes it's not even your body that makes you a boy or a girl. *It's how you feel inside.*" Might that message evolve over time? I hope so, if it means that we will continue to grow in our understanding of gender.

Part 2

TO BE A GRANDPARENT

Notes from a
Naming Ceremony

When Amaya was eight days old, we held a naming ceremony in our home. We invited family and friends to come meet the baby and offer their wishes for a healthful and happy life. We asked people to write their wishes for Amaya.

Here are two strikingly appropriate messages from that day, written by Amaya's paternal grandparents (emphasis added):

For Amaya

May your life be filled with constant discovery—of self, of life, of community, of world—and *always feel free to change that which you can change.*

Grandma Elaine

Amaya Jael,

I wish you happiness, and love, which I am sure you will have, and also *the daring and courage to become whatever you want to be*, which may be difficult and arduous at times, and even cost you some of that happiness that will come so easily but *may in the end be worth more than you think at first.*

Your Grandfather George

George died in 2020 and Elaine in 2023. May their memories always be a blessing.

They could not have known just how prescient these words were when they wrote them. Both before and after his transition, they each loved and supported and accepted their transgender grandchild completely. Their love will always be felt by those who remember them.

When I told my father-in-law George about my first book, *He's Always Been My Son*, he wrote this:

Dear Janna,

I've been trying to think of what I could say other than, of course, I support you and Amaya with all my heart. You, Janna, are brave and loving beyond my imagination, and I am always amazed at Amaya's cheerfulness and optimism despite the trials and anxiety he has gone through. And will face for many years to come. Assure him of all my love. (I will tell him myself when I see him.)

All my love,
Dad

George was not typically a letter writer, nor was he a man of many spoken words. His note above—and even more so, his actions—were born of his unconditional love and acceptance for his grandchild.

There are many ways to be a grandparent. Cultural and community norms and values may determine some of the roles a grandparent takes on within a family. Shifting norms and values may add challenges to some of these roles.

In addition to many functional roles (caregivers, breadwinners, homemakers, etc.), grandparents can be role models, inspirations, playmates, teachers, carriers of family stories, and so much more. But, let's face it, it isn't always easy to maintain the connections we so desire to have with our grandchildren.

"My grandchildren live so far away, it's hard to feel connected."

While some grandparents do live near their children and grandchildren, it is more and more common for families to be separated by geographic location. It can be difficult to stay connected, even with all the technology available to us. The physical distance between family members can also lead to a feeling of emotional disconnection. Grandparents can feel left out of or confused about their grandchildren's lives.

"I am being asked to use a new name and pronoun for my grandchild, and I don't understand what this is all about."

When a family member is exploring their gender identity or taking steps toward transition, grandparents who are not the primary caregiver often feel excluded or find themselves "in the dark" about the process. The responsibility to make decisions for the health and safety of minors principally belongs to their grandchildren's parent(s) or legal guardian(s). If the grandchild is already an adult, that responsibility is vested in the individual themselves. Grandparents are often presented with information about their grandchild's gender identity and then left to themselves to just "go along" and adjust on their own. It can be even more difficult to make adjustments if the grandchild is not in proximity and/or isn't open to talking about what is happening.

Sometimes, grandparents may even feel like they are trying their best to make adjustments, but then they are told they are "being hurtful" or "not adjusting fast enough." And, yes, everyone deserves some patience; certainly, these adjustments (like using a new name or new pronouns for your grandchild) are not always easy. But it is important that grandparents understand that pronoun or name mistakes can hurt, despite good intentions. It doesn't mean you are a bad person if you make mistakes—but perhaps understanding how hurtful those mistakes can be to your grandchild will provide you with additional incentive and underscore the urgency of the adjustments you need to make to show your love and give support.

Fran Wickner, PhD, MFT, a therapist with many years' experience working with trans individuals and their families, gave me this insight:

> I worked with one multigenerational family where the grandma lives with the family. But due to cultural and language barriers, the grandma wasn't privy to all that the child was going through with regard to being transgender and she didn't see the transition phase. So, when the grandchild transitioned, it took the grandma by surprise.
>
> Grandparents are often left out of the process. That can be really hard. They can feel really shocked as they don't get to see them moving through all the steps.
>
> Some teens have a hard time being patient with their grandparents as they are adjusting. Youth can be so defiant. They are used to everyone accepting them in their home community, and

though they know their grandparents are going to be shocked, they don't have much patience. They expect them to get their pronouns right every time. That is a challenge for grandparents.

More often than not, transgender people have been thinking about, exploring, and learning about their gender identity for a long time, often for years, before they share their feelings with family members. Using a new name and/or pronoun can be affirming, and these behaviors are often a significant contributing factor in relieving gender dysphoria. But the opposite is also true. Your grandchild may feel deeply hurt, more than just disrespected, when their former name or pronouns are used. They may appear impatient or even intolerant.

When trans people take a new name, it is a way of affirming their authentic self, the person they truly are. Some call their old or former name their *dead name*, meaning that the old name no longer has meaning to them. Transitioning to using a new name is a challenging adjustment for many grandparents. Perhaps that name may still hold deep meaning for you. It's okay to feel whatever you are feeling. In time, you will get used to the new name, and as you integrate your own experiences, you will see your grandchild for who they are, and that name will have meaning for you too.

Your grandchild may expect you to adapt right away to using their new name and/or pronouns, and it is important that you do adapt. This may take some time, and that is okay. It starts by *choosing* to adapt as quickly as you can, and doing whatever you can to realize that intention. Be patient with yourself as you are learning. Changing our brain patterns takes practice. Practice using the new name and pronouns until it becomes natural. In time, the new name and/or pronouns will lose its novelty and become "second nature." It may not be fast enough for your grandchild, but if you practice, they will notice. In most cases, it also will bring you closer together.

Adjusting to a new name and/or new pronouns takes practice. When my son transitioned, he kept the same name we'd given him at birth, but my husband and I (and many other people) had to adjust to using new pronouns. So, yes, I know from experience that it's not easy. But I also know you can do it!

SOME SUGGESTIONS FOR YOU TO PRACTICE

- Write a letter about what you like about your grandchild, or what you like to do with that person, using their new name and/or pronouns.
- Write sentences using your grandchild's new name and/or pronouns (like how we wrote sentences over and over on a chalkboard when we were kids).
- When you think about your grandchild to yourself, practice using their correct name and/or pronouns.
- Create a "pronoun jar"—like a swear jar. You put a dollar (or whatever amount you choose) into a jar every time you make a mistake. Perhaps you can tell your grandchild you are doing this, and maybe even let them decide what to do with the money. Or you can donate it to a local LGBTQ+ organization.
- Talk about your grandchild with other family members, friends, or even strangers. Speak fondly and positively of them using the correct name and/or pronouns.
- Proactively practice using your grandchild's new name and/or pronouns with a close friend or coworker, or another family member who is also trying to adapt. Agree to support each other in using the new name and/or pronoun, and to point out (nicely and briefly) when you slip up.
- Change your grandchild's name and/or add their correct pronouns in your phone's "Contacts" list, in other address books, on your birthday calendar, etc.

- Look through photos you have from previous years before your grandchild transitioned—and, while looking through them, say the person's correct name and pronouns to yourself. (Note: Some transgender people are okay with folks keeping old photos of them around, others are not. Many are okay with the family keeping them for private viewing only. If you are not sure, ask your grandchild.)

How will *you* practice? Take this opportunity to set an intention for yourself.

WHAT IF I MAKE A MISTAKE (AND YES, YOU WILL ALMOST CERTAINLY MAKE MISTAKES)?

- Do not make a big deal or make a big apology. It is important that you do not explain to the person why it is difficult for you. This only draws more attention to the mistake and puts the onus on your grandchild to then forgive you or take time to explain why it is hurtful or disrespectful.
- Take responsibility by quickly acknowledging your mistake, and then move forward by redoubling your effort to use the correct name and/or pronoun. For example, you might say, "She, I mean *he*, went to the store." (I have added emphasis here in print, but you should not emphasize the correct pronoun when you speak.)
- If you do find that you have been repeatedly misgendering your grandchild in a conversation, stop and regroup. Apologize (again, don't overdo it) and let your grandchild know that you know it is important to get it right. Assure them you will practice: "I realize I have not been using the correct pronouns for you. I will practice, and I will do better."
- Likewise, if you are talking with someone else about your grandchild and realize you have used the wrong name and/

or pronouns, briefly correct yourself and move on. "Juan—I mean Ana—is going to college next fall, I'm so proud of her." This behavior helps to model for others (and may help them remember to adapt to the new name and/or pronouns as well).

- Remember that "practice makes perfect." With patience and practice you will do better.

Another role for grandparents in many instances is to continue to be a parent to your adult children, the parents of your transgender grandchildren. Parents have much to navigate in order to provide the best support they can for their transgender children. As principal caregivers, they are the ones that must respond first and foremost to their children's needs. Parents of trans kids have to educate themselves—and sometimes educate the professionals in their children's lives—about the needs of transgender youth. Grandparents who are not primary caregivers for their grandkids are often witness to these decisions, but they are not the principal decision makers. That responsibility most often lies with the parents (who may be birth parents, adopting parents, or any other sort of legal guardian). These parents desperately need the support of *their own* parents. That's you, my dear grandparent!

Sometimes a grandparent is the main caregiver for a grandchild. If you are in that position, I encourage you to read books aimed at parents of transgender youth. These are just some of the great offerings out there for parents:

- *The Transgender Child* by Stephanie Brill and Rachel Pepper (Cleis Press, 2022)
- *The Transgender Teen* by Stephanie Brill and Lisa Kenney (Cleis Press, 2016)
- *My Child Told Me They're Trans...What Do I Do?—A Q&A Guide for Parents of Trans Children*, edited by Brynn Tannehill (Jessica Kingsley Publishers, 2023)

- And my first book, *He's Always Been My Son: A Mother's Story about Raising Her Transgender Son* (Jessica Kingsley Publishers, 2017)

A Grand Love, the book you are reading, also may be helpful for parents. Keep in mind, however, that this book is aimed mainly at grandparents who are not the main caregiver for their transgender grandchild. With that in mind, this book may be particularly useful and helpful for any parents, or any other family or community members, who are not the primary caregiver themselves.

Transgender people who struggle the most are those without support. Ideally, everyone would have the unconditional love and support of their parents and/or main caregivers, as well as their grandparents and their entire family. Unfortunately, this is not always the case.

The idea of having a transgender grandchild may be met with resistance from some grandparents or other family members. (For instance, you may be accepting and supportive of your trans grandchild, while other grandparents in the same family may not.) This can put a strain on relationships as the trans person, and the parents of that trans person, navigate their experiences.

Perhaps one might ascribe this resistance to generational differences. To a degree this may be true. However, I know grandparents in their 70s, 80s, and 90s who are their grandchild's #1 fan and ally, and for whom their love, support, and acceptance did not waver when they learned their grandchild is transgender. In fact, for some of the grandparents I know, it deepened their regard for their grandchildren, as you will read in some of the stories to come in this book.

Still, acceptance doesn't always come easy. When one person transitions, everyone in the family also experiences changes. The words one uses for someone may change; a *grandson* is now a *granddaughter* or a *grandchild.* Names and pronouns may change. There may be a sense of loss or even grief for some family members. Everyone's feelings are valid—and, at the same time, it can be helpful to explore where some of these feelings might be coming from. Whatever we were taught and shown about gender and the performance of gender plays a big part in how we respond to others with regard to gender.

Keep in mind that it is not the responsibility of your grandchild to help *you* process *your* feelings.

AN EXPLORATION—ASK YOURSELF

- What were the messages you received about gender while growing up?
- How did these messages create opportunities for you? Expectations? Limitations?
- Would you say that these ideas about gender had a generally positive or negative effect on you, or some of both, or neither?

We all have internal biases. Some are known to us, others are not. Learning that we have a transgender grandchild may bring us face to face with some parts of ourselves that take us by surprise. Some of our feelings may even make us feel ashamed.

"I didn't understand why I was so upset when I learned my grandchild was transgender. I thought I was a very accepting person."

Perhaps it is not so much a generational divide that determines how accepting we are of gender differences. Maybe what matters is whether we consider ourselves *lifelong learners*. What if we can open ourselves to new ideas? What if we can put aside our presupposed notions of what it means to be human? This is how we can begin to shift our expectations of who our grandchildren are "meant to be" and what their lives should look like. Perhaps then we can open a window to building a closer relationship with that person—and, I dare say, with all humanity.

One in 200

We did not know my son Amaya was transgender until he told us when he was in his teens. But during our early parenting years, we did know about someone else who had a transgender child.

According to a 2022 survey conducted by the Williams Institute,[1] one in every 200 people in the U.S. identifies as transgender. For ages 13–17, the Williams Institute's studies found the range of youth who identify as transgender varied from 1.8 percent in the Northeast to 1.2 percent in the Midwest. Also of note: the same study found that youth aged 13–17 are much more likely to identify as transgender (1.4%) than senior adults aged 65 and older (0.3%). It is also notable that the percentage of youth who identify as transgender has gone up significantly in recent years, while the percentage of adults who say they are transgender has stayed relatively the same.

In a similar vein, a 2022 Pew Research Center study[2] found that 1.6 percent of U.S. adults are transgender or non-binary. Among ages 18–30, that percentage rises to 5.1 percent. So, it shouldn't be a surprise that our family (or yours) would include a transgender young person. Indeed, as our society advances and trans people find more support in their communities and families, we are all likely to know more and more people who identify as transgender, especially more young people. But that was not the case even just a few years ago. Also from the Pew Research Center study: In 2017, roughly 37 percent of adults reported they know someone who is transgender. By 2021, that number had increased to 42 percent. Four in ten people now say they personally know someone who is transgender.

When Amaya was about five years old, in the earliest stages of expressing himself with male preferences for dress and hair, we found that we had a connection to another child who did not express gender in a typical way. That child was the granddaughter of one of my mother's close friends. Though the child's mother and I were also friends when we'd been kids, we had lost touch with each other over the years. Still, it was comforting to know that someone I knew, however distantly, also had a child who was gender non-conforming. I felt it was fortuitous that our mothers, the grandmas, shared this commonality and could support each other (and commiserate).

This other child, assigned male at birth, had insisted from 18 months of age that she was a girl. By five years old, after much research and counseling, her family decided to enroll her in kindergarten as a girl (her affirmed gender). Their daughter, Jazz Jennings, was the first transgender child in the U.S. (as far as anyone knows) to attend a public school with enrollment records reflecting her affirmed gender. In 2007, when Jazz was six years old, her family decided to go public, and they sat for an interview with Barbara Walters for the TV show *20/20*. Jazz and her family welcomed ABC's cameras—and the world—into their lives. She has since assumed the mantle of being a spokesperson and leader for her generation of trans youth. Her book *I Am Jazz* was a bestseller.[3] Written as a picture book suitable for children as well as adults, *I Am Jazz* tells the story of a transgender child, based on Jazz's real-life experiences. It was the first book of its kind to find its way into the public eye. My husband Gabriel and I were, and continue to be, inspired by the bold steps taken by Jazz's family in supporting and affirming their transgender child's true self.

When we heard about Jazz, I asked Amaya (who was about

eight years old at the time) if he wanted me to call him a boy. I told him it was okay with his dad and me if that's what he wanted, and that we loved him no matter what. But he said he didn't know. Whatever was happening on the inside, and however he appeared on the outside, he had not yet reached a stage in which he could affirm he felt he was a boy, certainly not verbally. In some ways, I just wanted him to declare a preference. It was hard to wait, to be in the unknown. But he was too young for me to think everything was settled. No matter what I thought I knew, and no matter how much I wanted my child to affirm what was becoming clear in my mind, I had to let him experience his own process.

My son and Jazz each showed what many consider early signs of being transgender. Jazz was more verbally insistent than Amaya was—but for my son, too, some of those early signs were always in view. There was not an *aha!* moment when I just knew my own child was transgender. As I have already said, my husband and I were keenly aware that our child was not your average "tomboy" (whatever that may be). Some of the signs we see today in our rear-view mirror include the way he insisted upon being dressed, the so-called "boy toys" he consistently chose to play with, and especially the way he carried himself and moved his body. It is important to note that these signs don't always mean someone is transgender. There is no one way to be a man, to be a woman, to be someone who is non-binary. Yet, looking back, we can see that the insistent, persistent, and consistent ways both Jazz and Amaya expressed themselves with regard to gender were early indicators that they could be transgender.

Even in those early years it felt like we were living in the in-between. People would ask if I thought Amaya's extreme version of tomboyish expression meant he would be a lesbian. (A conflation of sexual orientation and gender identity.) Or they would ask, "Do you think Amaya wants to be a boy?" I remember my mother once saying something like, "It seems pretty clear that Amaya likes to be seen as a boy, so maybe he does just want to be a boy."

I did not know then that one in 200 Americans identify as transgender. That figure alone might have pushed me sooner to a conclusion about my child or set us down a different path in our quest to support Amaya. At the time, my suspicions about my child's gender were hardening into a strong theory. But it would be quite some time before I reached out for resources.

Jazz and her family have shared their story of love, acceptance, and growth in many ways, including eight seasons (so far) of the TLC network reality TV show *I Am Jazz*. In doing so, Jazz has helped to shift the narrative about transgender children. The Jennings family has become a source of support for so many other families with transgender youth. Jazz herself has certainly been an inspiration to many transgender youth and their families—and also, there are quite a few transgender adults who have said they came to understand their own trans identity, and/or were inspired to come out and live as their authentic selves, because of Jazz's example. Jerni Edlon, author of *Jazz Mergirl* (CreateSpace Independent Publishing Platform, 2015), which is about Jazz Jennings and other transgender youth, says:

> After the publication of my book, I experienced a sudden and remarkable epiphany that I too am a trans girl. (Yes, I wrote the book before I even knew.) That was seven years ago, and ever since, I've been on an amazing, non-stop journey to Jerni!

Neither Jazz nor her parents knew their choice to become visible would be so influential. Families like mine are forever grateful to them.

Recently, I had the opportunity to interview Jazz's grandparents, Jacky and Jack. It was deeply inspiring to hear them tell their stories about how they came to understand, accept, and even celebrate having a transgender grandchild.

Here are some of the gems that shine out from our conversation:

Janna: Tell me about the early years with Jazz.

Jack: Jazz is fortunate in one sense: her grandfather [Jack is referring to himself] was trained as a physician and practiced medicine his entire career until he retired. This is a positive feature; having this kind of grandfather who doesn't look at the transgender issue as a stigma but as a challenge.

As a physician, I immediately looked at it as a challenge that has to be dealt with. I knew this immediately after familiarizing myself with the subject. I had the wherewithal to look these things up.

My first concern was that I knew there was a higher incidence of suicide.

It became a family issue. It was a challenge for us, as we knew it was a challenge for our grandchild. We knew there would be a very challenging time growing up.

Jacky: Early on, Jazz took a onesie, opened up the snaps, and said "dwess."

That's the way she saw herself.

Her mother had a tough time with her in preschool, and she held the line, advocating for Jazz even though others were skeptical. There will be people who are critical. Some grandparents might say, "What two-year-old or three-year-old is going to tell me who they are? You were born with this equipment, and this is who you are." And some have even said, "If my daughter told me this, I would give her a hit in the rear end and send her to the corner."

What does a grandparent do? As I grew up, I didn't know a gay person. We were thrown into this situation. As it became clearer and clearer, we realized we were not dealing with being gay, we were dealing with being transgender. I knew a bit about it just from reading or something like that.

Jack: From the beginning this was a mismatch.

Jacky: And we ran to catch up.

I remember my exact reaction when we spoke with the

doctors and professors. I was very upset. I knew it in my head and heart, but this confirmed it. It called for a period of reaching out for professional help to get me through the early times, and fast. Because in our personal situation, Jazz was moving along, Mom and Dad were moving along, siblings were moving along, and we who were not living with them had to catch up.

There was no choice. We were along for the ride. The first year was a crash course.

When we met with others, and those folks were floundering, we realized we could make a difference. We were educating, we did some lecturing, talking to groups, to a JCC [Jewish Community Center] group and to college groups, whoever wanted to listen.

We tried to spread the word, not an easy process. Everyone must deal with it in his or her own way. I had to do soul searching, and that was not so much of a challenge. It was just worrying about the world. I knew enough that once Jazz was labeled as transgender, this was not going to be an easy journey. It's a lifetime journey and does need the support of family and friends. If [grandparents] can move themselves along and get the professional help they need, they will catch up.

We were united as a family. We were learning along the way that there was no choice, this is a living human being. Gender is *boy* or gender is *girl*, that's the way it goes, and we were supportive. It was part of the entire experience, and we had to grow.

Jack said he had the benefit of being a doctor in his background. I didn't have that.

This was it, there was not a choice. And we certainly did deal with it. You are there for the family. You are there for your own child and you are there for that grandchild. For this family, there was no looking back.

Janna: What do you say to grandparents who do not see it that way?

Jack: They have to understand, you don't want to lose a grandchild.
Jacky: It happens.
Jack: My major concern was I wanted to have an *alive* grandchild.

Any grandparent that does not support and fully understand what is going on in the mind of a transgender person should not judge.

Back to basics in a way: When we evolve as a person, we know who we are from the very beginning. How you feel as a man or a woman, we know it is built into our psyche, our brains, and we know who we are from the beginning.

Jazz saw very early on she was a mismatch. It could've been a much bigger problem if she was unclear, but if you rate on one to ten, she was an eleven, she knew her body and brain was a mismatch.

It wasn't like we lost anything; we gained a "challenge."

We learned early on Jazz was exceptional in the way she could handle being transgender. It wasn't like a "woe is me" type of thing.

Jazz is very gifted and creative in poetry and writing—a lot of features about her that allow her to not go into the "woe is me."

My reaction is very closely related to Jazz's reaction.

Among the transgender population, the incidence of suicide is very high. If the person does not have family acceptance, the suicide rate immediately goes up. What are you going to do? Your family doesn't accept you, you don't feel your brain and body match, and you don't know what to do. It is better to have a living grandchild rather than someone who is subject to suicide. There is always that fear you are dealing with a potential suicide if a grandparent does not fully support the situation or doesn't understand what is going on in the mind of someone who is transgender.

Janna: Is it common for transgender people to come out early in life?

Jacky: Not all trans people come out early. Among those [trans-gender youth] we have met, the people who couldn't come out early were afraid, hidden.

Jack: Young people can now see themselves on TV. Our story [the *I Am Jazz* reality TV show] showed the world for the first time how a child grows up in a family that supports. And not only was she transgender, but she was on TV, showing the world, and young people were showing their parents: "This is me; this is how I feel." The show has helped people over time, with support and understanding.

Janna: Some trans people are afraid to come out to grandparents of your generation. What would be helpful?

Jacky: Education is the whole thing, even the program *I Am Jazz*. You have to ask grandparents if they would attend a meeting, do some reading, listen with their hearts and ears before mak-ing the final condemnation of throwing their grandchild away. Try to be part of it. Maybe they don't live nearby. Keep up with what's going on and try to hold on until they can accept, find acceptance for themselves. It takes a while. I was devastated— well, not exactly devastated, but I couldn't indulge myself. If they can, put their own discrimination aside and look for what the child needs, and try to make their life a little easier rather than getting caught up in your own needs.

Jack: Grandparents don't get to be the deciders. But we are the supporters, and we can do damage if we don't support. "We love you no matter who you are." Jazz always knew we were not the enemy.

It is better to have a living grandchild rather than someone who is subject to suicide. There is always that fear. This was not the major motivating factor for us *per se*, but it has to be a motivating factor to some extent because you are dealing with a potential suicide if a grandparent does not fully support the situation or doesn't understand what is going on in the mind of someone who is transgender.

Jacky: There are some grandparents who will never accept, and they are the losers.

Jack: There are some that don't support it, but that idea is foreign to me. I understand that exists, but when I look at Jazz, we love her, and we support her. And she loves us.

Jacky: This person is a human being. We don't throw away human beings.

Human beings *are* thrown away. There are some kids who do not have family acceptance, I call them the "throw away kids." They often turn to the streets to get what they want. They get hormones off the street or surgeries from unqualified people.

That is the whole sadness of this situation. So, in this moment, when things are so tough in politics and many other things, YOU DON'T THROW AWAY A CHILD!

You listen to the child, you listen to the parent, you listen to the family, and you get on board. And then you give all of yourself to the situation—and there's no ifs, ands, or buts about it, and that's the way we function.

* * *

"My grandparents are so special to me. When society rejected me for being transgender, they always provided me unconditional love and support. They may have grown up in a different era where transgender people were practically unheard of, but they dismissed the past and learned to accept me for who I am. I love them wholeheartedly and feel extremely grateful to have them in my corner forever. Everyone deserves grandparents like mine."

Jazz Jennings

Part 3

I LOVE YOU, NO MATTER WHAT

On Unconditional Love and Acceptance

My father, may he rest in peace, told me many times, "I love YOU, no matter what. I would never turn my back on you." And though he died before Amaya was born (in fact, while I was pregnant with him), I know that he absolutely would have loved and accepted his transgender grandson unconditionally.

At first, he would have been nervous, maybe even skeptical. He would have tried to learn what he could about what it means to be transgender. He would have reached out for answers. As a pharmacist, I know he would have wanted to learn about the medical aspects. He probably would have had some reservations and concerns, as there was little information available about supporting transgender youth when Amaya was young. But I am sure that when he learned about the risks of depression and suicidality for transgender people, he would have been motivated to support whatever we decided as Amaya's parents. He would have never turned his back, and I know my mother is right about my father; he would be proud of the man my son is today.

When humans are not familiar with something, we can easily go into fear mode. We are biologically programmed to do this.

Grandparents who learn their grandchild may be transgender, or who notice changes in their grandchild's gender expression, may feel trepidatious. A grandparent may be asking themself these questions:

"What does this mean?"
"Will my grandchild be safe?"
"What does this mean for me?"

It's okay to not understand. You can still love and accept and support your grandchild, even without (or before) understanding. Your grandchild needs you. Your love makes a difference, a vast and grand difference.

Perhaps the best place to start is to ask yourself this question:

"What does unconditional love mean to me?"

Some grandparents may say, "I don't care if you're transgender, I love you no matter what." People who say this mean well. They are trying to say they will be there, no matter who the person is, or what they do, or how they express themselves. These words are meant to be comforting and the intent is a positive expression of love. Yet, the impact of such words may not be received in the intended manner. Consider the possible impact of a phrase such as *I don't care if...* on someone who may be feeling very vulnerable. *I don't care if...* could push someone away even when the intention is to draw them closer.

I believe that if you are a grandparent, you almost certainly *do* care. In fact, you probably care very much. (You are reading this book, after all!) This deep feeling of care is likely at the root of any worry or fear you are experiencing. But sharing that feeling with your grandchild by saying *I don't care if...* is not supportive; despite good intentions, it is the opposite of supportive. Your grandchild needs to hear that no matter what, you *do* care, and you love them and support them fully. They also need you to get your own support. They need you to learn, to move beyond fear, to embrace this very personal part of them. They need you to accept their invitation to know them deeply and closely—and to show up with open arms, an open mind, and an open heart.

Sometimes, people may think they are being loving, but the impact of their words and actions does not reflect that love.

The two essays below were written by trans people who did not feel the unconditional love that every human needs. I am including them here to give voice to a common, unfortunate experience that countless LGBTQ+ people have reported after coming out to families that are nonaccepting. I am particularly grateful to these contributors for being willing to share their stories with us, as these accounts serve as cautionary tales as well as opportunities for us all to learn, self-reflect, and grow. If for some reason you see yourself reflected in these stories, offer yourself some compassion, and remember that it is never too late to change, to learn, to do better.

That Kind of Love Hurts

A Conversation with My Grandmother

JORDAN DECKER

It is my intention to always move from love and grace with my family around my transition from female to male. Here is an example of grace with my grandmother.

Set and setting is everything, so let's begin there.

It was March of 2017. My sister's husband had just passed away. I was six years into my transition. I had a full beard and had undergone "top surgery," a hysterectomy, and phalloplasty. Oh, and just to make it interesting, I also had a wrist and both elbows operated on for carpal tunnel and cubital tunnel syndrome. So, in a short time span of five years, I went under anesthesia ten times. (If you are interested, anesthesia and its effects on the body is an interesting topic to research.)

I had been with my sister all week. She was hardly sleeping or eating. All of her kids were around her. Our brother and our mom came as well. On this particular day, I was in my sister's kitchen with all of her kids. (Did I mention she has six?!) We were all helping to prepare a meal. My grandparents arrived, one of my nieces greeted them at the door. The first thing my grandmother did when she greeted me in the kitchen was use the wrong pronouns when she saw me. All of the grandkids just stopped, open mouthed, and looked at me.

At this time, I am six years into my transition. Again, I have a full beard, and unless I tell you I am a trans guy, you wouldn't know by looking at me. So, my grandmother directly looked at a man and *used the wrong pronouns*. I have had the privilege of passing since about six months on testosterone. I have been passing for *six years*! That's worth repeating to convey the level of frustration I have had to endure years into transition. People wonder why trans people have so many mental health diagnoses. We are traumatized and retraumatized every day through outright aggressions and microaggressions by the people who say they love us the most.

I quietly walked out of the kitchen and went into the living room to sit on the love seat. It had been six years—and still, she doesn't see me. I am hurt. I am unseen. Even though I was prepared for it, I am in shambles because this is happening again. The knife cut deep in my heart because I know deep down she loves me.

She comes into the living room and sits down on the love seat next to me. Yes, I chose to sit on the *love seat* knowing she would come sit next to me. Remember, I want to come from the most loving place I can for the following conversation:

Nanny: I've noticed you've pulled away from me, honey [the endearing term she has used for years with all of us grandkids].
Me: Nanny, you used the wrong pronoun for me in the kitchen.
Nanny: No, I didn't, honey.
Me: Nanny, when you did it, all of the kids turned and looked at me because they were afraid to correct you.
Nanny: I'm sorry, honey; it's only been three years, give me a break.
Me: Nanny, it has been six, and that kind of love hurts.

Nanny: Don't you pull away from me.

Me: Nanny, *that kind of love hurts.*

Nanny: I don't want to hurt you, honey.

Me: Then you know...

Nanny [she interrupts me]: I know, *that kind of love hurts.*

I never raised my voice. I didn't deviate from the mantra. I wanted to act, not *react*, this time seeing my grandmother. I wanted to be prepared to answer any of her comments in the most loving way that I could. Her interruption, saying she knows that the love she was giving hurts, was an amazing turning point for our relationship. I knew I was seen; I knew I was heard; I knew she still loved me.

I have experienced aggressions from other family members. My own mother didn't understand the wound caused by continuing to use the birth name and pronouns I used prior to transition. She went along with the family when I was not around, holding me to my past. We are not the same person at 40 as we are at 5, or 10, or even 25. We all grow and bloom into our most authentic selves over time. We just tend to judge those that are *too* different.

The next time I saw my mother, I told her the story of the conversation I had with my grandmother. She couldn't believe I stood my ground with *her* mother! Even writing this, I chuckle inside at my mother's reaction. She is in her early 60s and still has a hard time standing up to her mother!

The amazing thing was that my mother has heard me say, "If you don't practice when I'm not around, you'll surely make mistakes when I am around." Still, she was not using the correct name or pronouns when speaking with the family about me. *That kind of love hurts.*

Today, 12 years into my transition, my grandmother still uses the wrong pronouns on occasion. When it happens, I see the pain in her eyes for the mistake. Today, I am able to just overlook the mistake because I see she recognizes she has hurt me, and that hurts her. My mother can now call me her son; that journey is a whole other chapter for another book!

What I understand today is that we all have trauma patterns in our families. My mother was afraid to stand up to her mother regarding my chosen name and current pronouns for fear of rejection by her family—at almost 60 years old.

It's not my mother's fault I am transgender. It is my *gift* to be transgender. Every spectrum has a fulcrum, a middle. We all have gifts, and some of us are meant to balance the spectrum of gender.

Mother Earth moves in cycles. As humans, we are born to cycle. We are made to shift and change like the trees blowing in the wind. It is exhausting to continuously fight the constant daily micro-aggressions, from mispronouncing, to birth (dead) naming, to being asked inappropriate questions, to outright discrimination for being the human which I am created to be. How do I know this is who I am created to be? Because this is the human I am. Full of grace, full of heartbreaks, full of cycles.

Sometimes those of us that smile the biggest are hurt the deepest.

So, I ask you this: When speaking to a trans person, not to make it about you, or how hard it is for you to remember a new name or pronoun. Think about the human on the other side of your excuses. The hurt, the pain, the feelings of being invisible and unloved for whom they were created to be.

We are all spiritual beings on a human journey doing the best we can. As Maya Angelou says, "When you know better, do better." Forget beating yourself up or creating excuses for a pronoun or name mistake. Just respectfully apologize and move forward with grace. Where grace is given, grace will be received.

Thank you for reading a small part of my story. My human heart loves you for your willingness to understand that *different* is not good or bad, right or wrong; it's just not *the same*. I am grateful you are different from me so I can love more of the spectrum of being human.

My Poppa

DYLAN JACK JAMES

I always knew I was different. I couldn't quite put my finger on why, but it made sense to me later in life, much later. There were hints along the way. At age four, I loved pretending to shave with my grandpa. I started shaving my face again in adolescence until my best friend shouted at me, "What are you doing, girls don't shave their faces!" I hated playing with dolls or any girly toys. In 1978, at age 15, I came out as bisexual to my plastered-on-smile 1950s Catholic parents.

Back then, I was coming to terms with my sexuality and my gender, searching and contemplating what it meant for me. Telling my parents I was bisexual resulted in a Bible being thrust in my face by my angry father, along with his spit sermon on the prohibition against homosexuality contained in Leviticus. My mother was in tears, and I was now the black sheep of the family. My confession turned their Brady Bunch world upside down overnight. My mother's tears morphed into the fierce rage my father exhibited toward me.

Living at home proved unbearable. I ran away and became homeless. I ended up in a shelter for runaways and eventually was sent back home. The only kindness I had known as an LGBTQ teen was offered by a counselor at the shelter. I was persecuted severely by my mother and, after saving up enough money from a series of jobs, I moved out at age 18.

I had a child and reconnected with my family several years later, thinking they would want to meet their first grandchild. Things were fine for a while between us until my mom asked me if she could keep my son overnight. "It'll give you a break, I know how hard it is taking care of little ones!" she cooed in a loving voice. I should have been suspicious of her kindness after I told her my son and I were living with my girlfriend.

When I went to pick up my son the next day, they were gone. My mother had absconded with my two-year-old. I was tipped off by another family member who informed me that my maternal grandmother was in on the kidnapping. My grandmother refused to give me my child when I unexpectedly showed up at her apartment. My grandfather, whom I lovingly called my Poppa, became angry with his stubborn wife and intervened on my behalf. He insisted, "That's her child, you mustn't do this, give him to her!" (Note: I had not yet come out as transgender, and my pronouns were still *she/her*.) Only then was I able to get my son back. My aunt later told me that my mother had initially taken my son to Canada. She'd stashed him in a Catholic priest's house for a week prior to coming back to the U.S. and hiding him at my grandparents' apartment.

My aunt also shared with me how my Poppa had confronted my mom and grandmother and told them that what they were doing was wrong. He said, "These people can't help it, they're born this way!" He recommended leaving me and my son at peace to live our lives without family interference or worrying that my son would be affected in some negative way for being raised in a gay household. My Poppa became my hero, the only one in the family to come to my defense.

I later found out that he had worked with a lesbian woman for many years. He heard about her life experiences and understood that sexuality is innate. He was ahead of his time, having been born in 1906.

Fast forward to 2018. I was 56 years old, had raised two children, and buried a husband. I had developed severe depression and anxiety. I sought therapy. After much soul searching, I was diagnosed with gender dysphoria and started transitioning from female to male.

I spent close to a year in total isolation, sitting with my revelation, contemplating the outcome of telling my family. I wrote a four-page letter to my parents and was met with shunning and abandonment. I thought my transgender realization would bring things into focus for my parents and other family members. It did the opposite, angering them more than when I told them I was bisexual. I was met with deafening silence, unreturned phone calls, unread texts, shunning, and abandonment. My parents immediately cut me off from family gatherings. I spent, and continue to spend, all my birthdays, Thanksgivings and Christmases alone.

In my parents' eyes, being bisexual was bad enough, but changing gender was an unpardonable sin! At present, we speak, but only rarely. My new name and pronouns are utterly ignored.

(My grown sons also struggle to relate to me as a man. They tell me, "We don't know who Dylan is, we want our mom back!" It causes me great discomfort, and they think the term "parent" is weird. I have told them I am the same person inside, my heart has not changed, nor has my unending love for them.)

Becoming my true authentic self was an act of bravery. I modeled myself after my Poppa, who showed his courage when he stood up for me to my mom and grandma. Even though he and I never discussed that incident, just knowing that my Poppa understood me flipped a hopeful switch inside and shined a bright light inside my heart, which had been despondent for many years due to my unaccepting family.

To all the wonderful, loving parents and grandparents with transgender children and grandchildren: Please educate yourself on transgender people. Listen and learn from their lived experiences and their hearts. There is so much misinformation circulating about transgender people from social media, religious fundamentalism, political ideation, and social agendas. Research objective channels, and through your process walk hand-in-hand with your grandchild and learn together. Love them for who they are, not for who you wish them to be. Don't wait until they reach out to you; reach out to them first, and offer your grandchild the unconditional love, support, and acceptance they need.

I now love and see myself through the eyes of my dear Poppa, and I know I will always be okay just being me. He hugged my abandoned heart, and the memory of his unconditional love still finds its way to me in my loneliest and most difficult moments.

The Questions
We May Ask

The stories Dylan and Jordan tell are not uncommon. In fact, it is only recently that transgender people have decent odds (still far from good enough) of being accepted by their families and in society. Still, many trans people struggle to find their way without that acceptance. Regardless of how other family members respond, it is vitally important that grandparents provide and reflect unconditional love and acceptance to their trans grandkids. In fact, studies confirm that family support is the number one protective factor for transgender youth.[1]

Most of us have had unexpected experiences that rock our world and challenge everything we thought we knew about life. For many people, discovering they have a transgender, non-binary, or gender-diverse grandchild can be this type of world-rocking event.

We might say to ourselves:

> *"I didn't ever think this would be something I faced in my life."*

"I can't believe this is happening to me."

These are common responses I hear when I speak to grandparents who have just found out that their grandchild is transgender, non-binary, etc. Under the surface of these words, I sense shock, surprise, dismay, fear, confusion, expectation, and grief. It feels heavy.

Why is this shock, surprise, dismay, etc. a common response?

Consider this: transgender individuals historically in the U.S., and in most global cultures, have been marginalized, pushed aside, made invisible, shunned, violently attacked, and discriminated against in myriad other ways. Transphobia is deeply rooted in our culture, our communities—and, yes, within ourselves.

When someone we know comes out to us as transgender, it may be the first time we as cisgender people are learning about the challenges transgender folks experience. (Remember, *cisgender* describes people whose gender identity and sex assigned at birth are congruent, regardless of whether they identify as heterosexual, gay, lesbian, or bisexual.) Maybe it is the first time we directly and personally encounter *any* transgender person, as far as we know. Perhaps we have not had to think about transphobia with regard to ourselves or our family members.

Yet, the challenges transgender people experience have always existed. Trans folks have long suffered as a result of transphobia, the denial of transphobia, and the erasure of trans people (literally as well as figuratively) themselves.

With this understanding often comes the fear that our own family member may have to endure these horrendous challenges, and perhaps also a fear that we, the grandparents, will suffer in any number of ways as a tangential result.

For someone to say, "I didn't ever think this would be something I faced in my life," when talking about having a child or grandchild who is transgender, it just means that it never dawned on the speaker that their child or grandchild would be anything but cisgender. Similarly, a person might say the same thing when they find out their child or grandchild is gay, lesbian, or bisexual; the notion simply never crossed their mind. A follow-up thought in either case might be, "I always assumed this is something that happens to *other* people's children; it never occurred to me it could happen to *my* grandchild."

I can relate. When I was pregnant, I was certainly aware that one day my child might say, "Mom, I'm gay." (Certainly, not all parents and grandparents share my awareness even about that.) Yet, I didn't have any inkling that my child could be someone who is transgender. Why not?

I was ignorant. I didn't know what I didn't know. At that time, I didn't know much about being transgender. I had never met anyone who was transgender, at least as far as I knew at the time. I certainly didn't know that children could be transgender. I did not have exposure to any positive transgender role models, and I had not been exposed to trans people in the media or in my school, work, and social experience. Trans folks were just not part of my world—or so I thought.

Now I know that transgender people are a part of all sorts of communities in all states and countries, in all societies and cultures throughout the world. Transgender people are humans. And as such should they have the same rights as people who are not transgender.

Sadly, this is hardly the case in much of the world. It is far too common for transgender people to be denied the same rights as people who are not transgender.

Transgender people all around the world have families. And many have not been welcomed by their families, by their communities, and by their regional/national societies as a whole.

What are some of the root causes of this global situation?

- Historic lack of visibility of trans and non-binary people in society, media, positions of leadership, etc.
- Lack of acceptance
- Cultural/religious beliefs
- Myths and disinformation about trans people and about what it means to be transgender
- Political forces that use transgender people as pawns ("They are coming for your children!")

There is, however, some good news. Today, there is more visibility for trans people than ever before. And along with this visibility has come increased and growing acceptance of transgender people—perhaps lagging several years behind acceptance of "LGB" individuals, as I discussed earlier, but certainly moving ever so slowly in the right direction. In fact, given the visibility and (in many regions and cultures) growing acceptance of LGBTQ+ people in almost every corner of the globe, it would be reasonable for parents and grandparents today to recalibrate their inner dialogue:

"I wonder if my child/grandchild will be trans? Or gender expansive? Or gay, or heterosexual, or any of the other wonderful variations of being human? Just like how I wonder if their eyes will be brown or if they will like strawberry ice cream."

Intersectionality

Sadly, we also see new challenges emerging or gaining in significance as visibility increases.

Each person has their own set of strengths and challenges. Challenges can be confounded by a person's individual layers of intersectionality. The term *intersectionality* was coined by Kimberlé Crenshaw to help explain the oppression of African-American women.[2] Intersectionality refers to the ways inequalities with regard to race, class, culture, religion, gender identity, sexual orientation, and other elements of a person's identity layer over each other and impact that individual.

To understand intersectionality, consider first that in the U.S. and elsewhere, people of color do not have the same privileges as White people. People of color are far more likely to experience discrimination and institutional racism in many ways. This is not because of something a person has done, but simply because of the color of their skin.

The concept of intersectionality describes how a person who is, for instance, Black and trans (there are many other types of intersectionalities, of course) is burdened by multiple layers of challenges that compound each other. Using mathematic symbols, we might describe these challenges as a sum where 1+1=3. If a person is also of lower economic status, that adds yet another compounding layer. The intersectionality of these aspects (in this example, being Black, trans, and poor) makes it significantly more challenging to just *be* in this world—to find housing, employment, access to medical care, and, above all, just to live as one's true self.

Intersectionality does not mean that a person assuredly will not be successful in life, won't find adequate housing, won't find employment, and cannot gain access to medical care. But it does mean that multiple layers, or *intersections*, of inequality and disparity are likely to lead to significant and intensified challenges for a person based on factors that person cannot change.

Intersectionalities for trans people (or for anyone, but here we are focusing on trans people) may also include physical or mental illnesses, disabilities, or other types of impairments and body/mind differences.

It is interesting to note at this point that there is an observable documented correlation (but no evidence yet of causality) between neurodiversity, which includes autistic people, and gender diversity. In one study, data show that people who do not identify with the sex they were assigned at birth are three to six times as likely to be autistic as cisgender people are.[3] (It is important to understand that autism is not considered a mental illness. It is a developmental condition, a type of neurodiversity, that affects how people see the world and how they interact with other people.) Certainly, this correlation does not mean most trans people are autistic or otherwise have neurodiverse characteristics. For those who do share this intersectionality, however, they may experience unique challenges.

One grandmother sent a message to me recently that touched on this notion of intersectionality. While none of her grandchildren are both autistic *and* transgender, her perspective is both novel and encouraging regarding the uniqueness of all humans and our myriad variations:

Between us, my partner and I have seven grandkids aged from five to nineteen. Two are autistic, two are transgender. Isn't that

A Grand Love

fascinating? This has caused me to theorize that neurodiverse and gender-diverse kids are the growing edge of our species. They are humanity trying to adapt and evolve to survive this unique predicament on our planet. So instead of worrying about them, I thank them and honor them and cheer them on for their strength to be born and be themselves at this exact moment in history.

It's Not "What You Believe"

Many people who discriminate against transgender people say they do not "believe" in people being transgender. This is akin to not believing in people being tall, or deaf, or left-handed. Of course, people who say this deny they are discriminating in any way, but a denial does not eliminate the discriminatory effects of their "belief."

The science regarding *why* gender diversity exists remains unsettled for now, but the consensus of the American Psychological Association, the American Academy of Pediatrics, and many other scientific bodies confirms that gender diversity is a variation of being human which exists across all cultures and regions and has persisted for all time. In this book, I accept and adhere to the broad consensus of scientists who have studied gender diversity; for me, it is a "given." But for those who want to explore the relevant science and related topics in depth, a good place to start is the book *Everything You Ever Wanted to Know about Trans (But Were Afraid to Ask).*[4]

Some people today want to legislate what levels of gender-affirming care people can access for themselves or their children. Some want to use the law to deny gender-affirming care completely, either for children or for anyone at all. But most of these people evidently have no clue what it means to be transgender, and they are ignorant of the real-life impact of such legislation on people who need but are denied access to gender-affirming care. They "believe" there is something wrong with allowing humans to vary from some preconceived norm. They "believe" it is immoral, evil, or dangerous to allow children to express themselves and live authentic lives that reflect their true gender identity. They deny the wide body of behavioral, medical, and psychological science that supports providing appropriate gender-affirming care. They deny the large body of evidence which shows that withholding this care leads to unacceptable rates of depression and suicide, particularly among trans youth.

Most likely, these people have not directly (or even indirectly) experienced the challenges, discrimination, and violence that transgender people encounter in our world today. They have not had to respond to a child who is beside themselves with fear about which bathroom they can use, or whether they will be mis-gendered once again today, or how they cannot reconcile their incessant, deep feeling that they were born in the wrong body. Perhaps the people who support legislation prohibiting gender-affirming care have not had to hold their child in the middle of the night for fear they won't wake up with their child still in this world tomorrow. Almost certainly, they are not among the many thousands of parents and grandparents who have lost a child or grandchild to suicide resulting from a lack of family acceptance. Nor have they had to console a parent or grandparent following such a devastating and needless loss.

Some people say, "I don't believe being trans is a *thing*." But saying this does not make being trans go away. It is most definitely a *thing*.

Even those who *do* understand that gender diversity exists might tell themselves, "I didn't ever think this would be something I faced in *my* life." But this apprehension displaces what *should* be a parent's or grandparent's primary concern. Such notions are only self-reflective and not very helpful (although it is always worth acknowledging to oneself how we feel). A grandparent's primary concern should always be for their trans grandchild, who in all likelihood will face at least some significant challenges in their life regarding their transness. These challenges will outweigh a grandparent's inner turmoil regarding their own willingness to accept these kids for being their authentic selves.

Grandparents need to recognize that many people in society will hate their grandchild; that their grandchild likely could face significant discrimination, including legislative and systemic discrimination; that they may face personal encounters that range from embarrassing to devastating to violent. All of that just because they are who they are.

So, yes, there is a lot to be concerned about. But it's not about *you*, it's about *them*. Our transgender children and grandchildren do not have the privilege to ignore those challenges. As parents and grandparents, we honor, love, respect, and help our children by sharing those concerns—and by helping to change the world to ensure that their safety and success outshine the "beliefs" of those who stand in their way.

One of the most common responses I hear when I tell transgender people about the work I do as a coach, author, and educator, and about being a supportive parent of a trans son, is a variation of, "I really wish that I had a family that would have accepted *me*." As we know, too many transgender people are not at all accepted by their families.

Countless transgender youth (as with many other LGBTQ+ teens) are kicked out of their homes, or feel they have to leave because they feel unsafe at home. Recent studies tell us that 25 percent of homeless youth today identify as LGBTQ+. Many of these kids are afraid to identify themselves as such, so the number is most likely higher.[5]

How is it that a parent or grandparent can turn their back on their very own child/grandchild? I truly cannot fathom this.

I implore you: *please* don't be the cause of your grandchild's suffering. *You can do this*, regardless of your age, your culture, your beliefs.

You *can* adapt, and you *are not* alone.

It bears repeating:

Being transgender is just one more beautiful normal variation of being human. Every child deserves to be loved and supported unconditionally.

The essays that follow provide examples of grandparents who offer unconditional love. *A Grand Love* indeed.

Grandparents and Transgender Grandchildren

JOHN KAUFMAN, GRANDFATHER OF A
TRANSGENDER GRANDCHILD, AND EDUCATOR

When I first began thinking about this topic, and about how I could describe the way I feel about living with a grandchild who made such a momentous decision, I immediately jumped to the image of the proverbial *before* and *after* picture. The *before*: a budding adolescent. Zoey was shy, quiet, and seemed trapped in a state of emotional limbo. Zoey was unhappy with school, withdrawn, and unsure. The *after* picture shows Patrick; a confident, creative, pragmatic, thoughtful, happier person. When he says, "I love you, Papa," it melts my heart.[6]

When Zoey first announced to me and her mom and sister that she wanted to be called Patrick, I accepted her decision. I didn't truly understand her desire for change and just saw it as a phase. She was reticent about explanations to anyone besides her mother. To her divorced father (my former son-in-law), she was still Zoey. My daughter was fully supportive of the change.

When my daughter invited me to join her in a local support group for families of transgender children, I attended a few sessions. I began to hear about the variety of experiences families were having and the spectrum of reactions to the transgender pronouncements by their trans kids. Some families get upset, fractured, obsessed. Some are able to rally in unpredictable ways.

During this period of change, I saw Patrick regularly. At first, it felt like I had to learn the rules of a new game. Sometimes I forgot to use "Patrick" and "him." He questioned regular schooling and still seemed withdrawn. Yet, I knew internal stuff was happening, and I wanted a way in. He started writing stories that he let me read. A deeper connection and understanding of the depths he was exploring washed over me. He was communicating so much through his fiction about things I had no idea about. We grew closer.

I read about transgender youth and viewed several video interviews with transgender high school students. Patrick was in the process of enrolling at an independent high school program. The contrast between the politically active and assertive students in the interviews I watched and the quiet way Patrick presented his change in public was stark. I had to address my expectation that Patrick should announce boldly to the world who he was becoming. I have since learned that kind of demonstration just isn't him. After high school, Patrick learned how to drive, and he now has a steady job that he takes seriously.

In the evolution of Zoey to Patrick, I have been a witness to his positive growth toward a knowledge of self and a more comfortable sense of being in the world. Struggling with confusion as a teenager is common; coming through this time of molting and emerging as a happier, more grounded person is not so common. I believe that this process for him always includes thoughtfulness, consideration for others, and a sort of restraint that helps protect his equanimity.

I just keep on loving and encouraging him to do what feels right.

An eagle's-eye view of what I have experienced might look like a series of forks in the road that required dedicated choices on my part. Patience versus quick judgment. Understanding versus feigned ignorance. Unconditional love versus bargaining. Acceptance versus emotionally backed expectations. Trust versus fear. And finally, arriving at a destination of *love* that wants the best for your treasured grandchild. I believe my choices have supported Patrick's growth and well-being.

Observing Patrick's transition has stretched my thinking about gender roles and one's sense of self. First of all, I believe that being in a free society should allow any of us to explore our personal depths as long as it causes no harm to others. Second, if we accept and understand that the freedom to choose whom we love is a basic right, then it should follow that we have a right to choose how we love ourselves.

I Am My Grandpa's *Eynikl*

ELI TEEL

Due to generational differences, it sometimes can be particularly hard for grandparents to understand their grandchild's experience with gender. I was lucky enough to have grandparents who made an active effort to understand what I was experiencing by asking me questions and even attending an LGBTQ+ family support group. The approach they took was that although they might never be able to understand why I transitioned, they would support me regardless.

Every supportive presence in a trans person's life, especially for trans youth, makes a big difference. Respecting a person's preferred name and pronouns is a great place to start.

When I first came out to my grandparents and started transitioning, my grandpa taught me a Yiddish word, *eynikl*, which means *grandchild* and has no associated gender. Sharing this with me showed me that he sees me for who I am, and that regardless of my gender, he will always love me first and foremost as his grandchild.

This sums up one of the most important things that a trans kid needs to hear: *your value to me is not contingent upon your gender identity.*

The Same One I'd Loved

JACKIE C

This child was the same one I'd loved from the moment he took his first breath, and that love would never change.

The most rewarding part of becoming a parent is becoming a grandparent! I love all three of our sons and feel fortunate that even though we've had some real challenges, we've remained a very close family.

I came from a difficult background with parents who were typical of those times. I was born in 1943, when they were in their late 30s and early 40s. My parents had limited experience with people who were different from them in any way. I suppose I could have grown up with the same narrow views, but I feel grateful that for some reason, I always accepted others for just who they were. I had no idea how much that attitude would serve me.

Our youngest son didn't marry until he was 36. We were beginning to wonder if he would ever settle down. He and his wife chose 07/07/07 as their wedding date, and we were blessed to find out the following February that they were expecting a child. I was included in the development of the pregnancy and invited to attend the ultrasound appointment where they were told they would be having a little girl. After having three sons and one grandson, I was thrilled to think we could finally start having tea parties at grandma's house in the years ahead.

The day arrived with an early call on November 8, 2008. Election Day. My daughter-in-law, being the trooper she is and already in labor, went out to vote before returning home to prepare for a home birth. She and my son had invited three people to attend the birth that day: her mother, her best friend, and myself. It was so amazing to watch my son and his wife go through the process of bringing this perfect little child into the world together with gentleness and love. They lived in a rural part of our community, and I would drive out to their house almost every morning to sit with this child on my lap and just stare in wonder at her little face. I believe because I had that opportunity, a deep and special bond was formed. Two years later, they had another little girl, and now we were really set to have some dress-up days as well as tea parties. And we sure did!

As time went on, there were a few signs that something was distressing the oldest child. Lots of emotional acting out, and some very sad days of real upheaval in their home. Looking back, so much makes sense now. But at that time, none of us had any idea what was happening. In August of 2020, that little girl told her mom that she felt she was not a girl and wanted to be a boy. My daughter-in-law is one of the most open-minded people I've ever known, and I couldn't pick a more perfect set of parents than she and my son to help this child know they were loved and accepted from the very beginning of this realization.

To say I was surprised is somewhat of an understatement. The hardest part was learning that he no longer wanted any photographs of his earlier years and didn't want his birth name ever mentioned again. He told us that he felt that child was dead. We had just lost our oldest son to cancer a few months before this, and now I felt we were mourning the loss of the first little girl in our family. Our hearts were broken. But I knew immediately that I would do anything asked of me to support this child.

This child was the same one I'd loved from the moment he took his first breath, and that love would never change.

Then began the education of pronouns and gender identity as well as sexual orientation, and not getting all of those things confused. I feel so happy that I live in a community that provides support for the LGBTQ+ people in our area. I learned that there was an online grandparents' support group organized by The Spahr Center, a non-profit organization in our county that provides support and resources for LGBTQ+ youth and families (along with other community services). This support group was a forum where grandparents could come together to learn about this whole new world that I personally was not previously aware of. Participating in this group has helped in remarkable ways and has taught me how to be sensitive to my grandchild, as well as to my son and his wife. We are all still learning as we grow together on this continuing path of love and understanding. I feel truly blessed.

Part 4

NAVIGATING THE JOURNEY FROM DISCOVERY TO ACCEPTANCE

According to the American Academy of Pediatrics, most children have a stable sense of their gender identity by the time they are four years old. This is true for all kids, regardless of their gender.[1]

In their 2023 study, one of the largest randomized samples of U.S. transgender adults to date, the KFF/*The Washington Post* Survey Project found that, "Most trans adults say they knew when they were young that their gender identity was different from the sex they were assigned at birth." The study found that, "About a third (32 percent) say they began to understand their own gender identity when they were 10 or younger, and another third (34 percent) realized it between the ages of 11 and 17." However, inner knowing doesn't mean someone will share this information with anyone. The study also reported that, "Three in 10 say they began telling others they were trans before the age of 18, while about a third (32 percent) came out between the ages of 18 and 25. Others came out later, and 12 percent of trans adults have not told anyone."[2]

Trans people describe this space between self-realization and outward expression as a time often marked by confusion, fear, and even shame, with little support from families or schools.

There is no one way to be transgender, and there is no single trajectory for all transgender people's lives. Each person is unique, and each person's experience is unique.

It is common for transgender and gender-questioning people to experience different levels or degrees of gender dysphoria over time. As each person resolves one layer of dysphoria, other layers may be revealed. Consider this: the journey of discovery and healing is not unique to transgender people; it is a common experience among those who undergo any process of self-discovery and healing.

Humans are multilayered beings. There is the surface layer, the part of us we show to the world, the part the world sees. There is our inner world, our layers of thoughts and feelings. There is our subconscious layer, our dream world. There is our DNA, layers and layers of genes passed down from generation to generation. There are layers of ourselves created by our personal perceptions, layers of experiences we hold in our memory cells, experiences that influence our physical forms, our thoughts, our emotions, and our responses to our experiences. Behind all of these layers are unknown parts, secret even to ourselves. And, at our deepest core, we will find the unwavering truth of who we are. (For many reasons, many of us never reach this core layer, but it's always there.) If we choose to do the work, we can peel back these many layers and uncover our deep truths.

Who are we? How do we know?

Most humans never embark on this oftentimes arduous (and only sometimes joyful) journey of self-discovery. For some, including my transgender son, Amaya, the need to peel back the layers and fully reveal and affirm their truth is overpowering and compelling.

12-2-08

I am unique because I am a girl dressed as a guy. I also act like a boy. Every time I meet someone new they think I am a boy. That is why I am unique.

"I am unique because..." (Written by my son, Amaya, when he was ten.)

A Swishy Boy

CASSIE BRIGHTER, WRITER, PUBLIC SPEAKER,
AND GENDER EDUCATOR

I was aware I wasn't a boy since I was very young. I yearned to be one of the girls, but that path seemed denied to me. My grandfather, a stern, highly religious Russian Orthodox Bible scholar, was quite fond of me—and he was uncomfortably aware I was a very "swishy" boy. I remember him cautioning me, in the most careful wording, that there are men in this world who are attracted to "boys like me." And that I should be careful of such men.

I understood the warning, and I fully understood—and embraced—the idea that grown men should not mess around with youngsters. But there was also something thrilling in knowing that there were men out there who could find me attractive. Just like a ten-year-old girl dreams of someday blossoming into a sexy woman, ten-year-old me longed to someday be looked at the way men looked at Betty Boop or Marilyn Monroe.

But I loved my grandpa and valued his approval, so I did my best to hide any vestige of girliness when I visited him.

This wasn't the only context where I learned to give up pieces of me, hide pieces of me. My father and his buddies would gather by the barbeque on weekends, telling jokes. It was like a rap battle, the men outdoing one another, aiming for the biggest laugh.

But each of those jokes was misogynistic, racist, homophobic, transphobic. As a nine-year-old, I learned through those jokes who belonged in the community—who was well thought of, and who was unworthy, lesser than, undesirable. Pitiable. Mockable. At night, as I said my prayers, I asked God to please not let me be "one of those."

When I finally came to terms with my transgender nature in my forties, it wasn't the blossoming that some trans kids get to experience today. It was an admission of defeat. It was a surrender. After four decades of trying to comply with the imperative of "be a man," I finally was ready to say, "I just can't do it anymore." I had spent far too long hiding so much of me. This creates a deep shame wound because I knew the most real part of me was detestable, unworthy. And the part of me everyone praised was an act, a puppet show.

Even then, my first thought was, "Fine, I'll take this to my grave, and no one will ever know." It took many years of pain and uncomfortable growth to start loving myself—the self I had been hiding for decades.

Recently I had a dream Grandpa had come to dinner, and I was at the family table. As I got up to hug him in my dream, I became aware of my breasts—and I was overcome with a deep panic, realizing he didn't know of my transition. I woke up in a cold sweat.

Grandparents often play a huge role in a child's life. I saw my grandfather as a gentle patriarch, a wise man, a connection to my heritage. His approval meant everything to me. And I guess it still does.

My Personal Story

WILL VARGAS

Growing up in a small town means everybody knows you or knows of you. My relationships with my friends and family are strong, and these people have been there for me throughout my entire journey.

I've known who I want to be my whole life, but I never knew where to begin. On January 19, 2019, I came out to my family as a transgender male. The fear of not being accepted sat with me for so long. My original intention was to wait until my final year of high school, or until I was an adult, before coming out. I was feeling so deeply uncomfortable in my own skin, I couldn't continue to live with myself. I am so pleased to say that I've never been more content with the choices I made five years ago.

My name is Will Vargas, and I am here to share my story.

I remember wanting to be just like my younger brother when I was four. I used to go into his room and beg to wear his T-shirts. Eventually, I started asking my mother to shop in the little boys' department. I've always dressed in mostly masculine clothing, and for the majority of my life, I was viewed as a tomboy. I spent my time at elementary school socializing with boys and never had an issue when waiters or waitresses assumed I was a boy.

As soon as I entered middle school, I withdrew from associating only with a friend group made up entirely of boys because of the sports I played. Alongside men's baseball and women's softball, I also participated in women's basketball, soccer, track and field, and cross-country. I was part of a close-knit group of friends connected through sports, and I remain in contact with those friends today. There were many times while participating in women's sports when people or other teams thought it was unfair for a boy to be playing on a women's sports team. This generated a subtle pressure in me to meet an expectation in society, and that was to dress and act more female so nobody would be confused any longer. In the eighth grade, I came out as bisexual to my friends and family, then several weeks later, as a lesbian. As long as I can remember, I have had a sexual attraction to women, but admired men and had the desire to become one.

When I hit high school, I had a good idea as to what I wanted for my future, although I was clueless when it came to starting my process. I decided to write a letter that I would soon read to my family. Coming out this time was one of the hardest things I have ever done, but I felt as if a weight was finally lifted after all that time. I took my time telling each of my friends, but adjusting to this whole new chapter in my life while in school wasn't easy. Those who didn't know still used my dead name and incorrect pronouns, which took a toll on me. I soon decided to continue my education through homeschooling.

I began taking hormones, starting with a very low dose, on March 5, 2019. I had a relatively late onset of puberty, but since I never fully experienced female puberty, I was able to start testosterone without a hormone blocker. Then, on July 29, 2019, with the help of my wonderful family and doctors, I underwent top surgery. I can still vividly remember the sensation of utter bliss that surged through my body as soon as I awoke from that operation. The way my transition had begun, I had the impression that I was in a dream. I am incredibly grateful to be so fortunate and have had support along the way.

I decided to return to campus to complete my senior year of high school after spending the first three years at home improving myself. Everyone was calling me Will at this point and using he/him pronouns. I became more confident in myself, and I felt more at ease using the male restrooms and being in class. During my senior year, I made my first male best friend. Ever since then, my family, friends, and classmates have shown me so much love and support.

As I grew more at peace with myself, I became aware of how little help I was receiving from people who were experiencing similar things. In high school, I only had one transgender friend whom I would occasionally talk to about various topics, but we were never particularly close. I attempted to join a group for LGBTQ+ youth that met about an hour away from my home so I could talk to people who might have experiences to share or knowledge I could use to help me get through this continuing process. I was very anxious about being with individuals I had never met, and this gathering was far away. I told my grandma that I couldn't do another session, and I explained that I felt lonely not having peers I could relate to closer to home.

Then on May 7, 2019, my grandma Jeanne Vargas decided to start CoastPride,[3] a non-profit organization in my hometown for LGBTQ+ youth and adults from all over the area where we live. I've been able to meet a lot of new individuals through Coast-Pride, and I've also had the opportunity to volunteer at several lovely local events. CoastPride has now partnered with the school district where I grew up to educate students and staff on how to make students feel safer at school. My grandmother has created an amazing outlet in my hometown, and I am extremely excited to see what the future holds for CoastPride and our wonderful community. I am so proud of her for all her time and dedication to making it the best center on the coast.

I would like to offer advice to grandparents of transgender individuals who are trying to understand their grandchildren.

To start, having an open heart and mind is beneficial for a conversation with your grandchild that involves their feelings of vulnerability. Open hearts and minds create a feeling of comfort. Actively listening to your grandchild is also important when questions come up throughout your process of understanding. I remember how difficult it was to be clear when explaining to my grandparents what I wanted, but they gave me the time and space to finish talking before asking questions or interrupting. They made me feel heard and presented unconditional love no matter what my choice was.

At this most recent point in my life, as I look back on my experience through this transition, being who I am saved my life. Without my grandma, I don't know if I would be here today.

Few people realize that letting others be who they are and giving them the support they need can actually be lifesaving.

I realized during my teenage years that I still didn't know what I wanted and how much change to expect. To this day, I struggle with comparing myself to other cisgender men in hopes of passing as one. I have faced that all my life, and all our lives are ever-changing, even if you might think something has ended. I have always longed for my transition to be speedy, and at times I still struggle with the fact that I am (still) going through puberty slower than others. With as much social anxiety as I have, social norms have unfortunately influenced me to lean away from being true to my authentic self. Now that I am starting my second year of college, I have been doing much better in my attempts to love my true self while also receiving help from both of my loving grandmothers along the way.

Now I am 19 years old. I have been Will for about five years. Since I'm now an adult, I've started increasing my hormone dosage and getting used to scheduling my own appointments and prescriptions. I've been putting in a lot of effort at school while enjoying my second year of college and working a part-time job. I am still receiving support from my amazing friends, my family, and my wonderful girlfriend while living at home. My parents have been a huge support to me during this journey, and words cannot express how thankful I am for them.

If I could go back in time, I would encourage the younger me to stay strong and keep going. I would tell myself to remember to maintain your determination and take it day by day. Great things come with time, so don't give up on yourself, and seek help whenever you may need it.

On Coming Out

Longtime colleague Cammie Duvall, a Licensed Marriage and Family Therapist with expertise working with LGBTQ+ youth and their families, has some wise words for us:

> Coming out is actually letting people *in* on very personal and intimate information. It can be less overwhelming to think of disclosure as an invitation in rather than a coming out. Each person gets to decide who they let in and when they let them in.
>
> Coming out can be a very lonely process. No matter how much support one has, letting people into one's most inner world is a vulnerable and courageous act.

Many transgender people take a gradual approach to transitioning and coming out. People who have shared their own stories with me concur this is common. It is noteworthy that in many of the stories I have heard and read, trans people report that they felt deep concern about the impact of their transition on other people in their lives. The following is a collection of some of the thoughts that might add to one's challenges during transition:

"I don't want to make things hard for them."

"I don't want her to worry if she makes a mistake."
"I don't want to draw attention to myself."
"How will they react?"
"Will she still love me?"
"Will I be safe?"

Exposing our innermost thoughts and experiences to others calls for bravery and vulnerability. Coming out is risky! Some people face unaccepting friends or families. Some trans and gender-diverse youth are kicked out of their homes before they are even 18. Trans people may experience violent reactions to their transition, perhaps becoming victims of "hate crimes" (crimes committed against people based specifically on animosity towards their identity or ancestry), including assault, rape, and murder. Many will suffer discrimination or bullying at school or in their workplace. It can be challenging or impossible in some states and communities for trans people to get necessary medical care, or other types of gender-affirming care, and/or insurance coverage to pay for those services.

These risks will remain significant until our society is more understanding and accepting of gender differences. Sadly, we have a long way to go. So, it's no surprise that many people choose to take baby steps and move slowly through their transition with a reluctance to reveal themselves to some audiences.

Not coming out has risks as well. For many trans people, the many secrets they have to keep may at some point become a bigger burden than the risk of coming out. It can be very stress-ful, painful, and isolating to live a life other than one which is authentic and true to one's inner sense of self. Doing so can have devastating consequences. We know that transgender youth and young adults are at disproportionally high risk of depression, anx-iety, suicide, and self-harm. As I wrote earlier, we know that trans people who report the highest rates of success and happiness in their lives are those who say they were able to transition and live as their authentic selves with the support of their families and communities.

Grandparents are typically not the first to know. Sometimes, it can feel like they are the *last* to know. Many parents and grandparents feel the information comes out of nowhere. They may say, "There were no signs."

Or they may think, "This seems very sudden." But the fact is that most transgender people have thought about their gender identity for a very long time, perhaps for their whole lifetime, before inviting others in.

Each person will have their own timeline for coming out and their own reasons why they take their time inviting people in. As I've mentioned several times, it can be a daunting process. If a person is worried about how someone else will respond to information about their gender identity, it may take them some time to invite that person in. While a grandparent cannot force the unfolding, they can take some tangible steps to make it more likely that their family member will invite them in.

Grandparents must do their best to be receptive, available, and open. One very important thing we can all do is to get educated on what it means to be transgender or non-binary. Even little things matter. Some folks might try to show acceptance of LGBTQ+ people by flying a pride rainbow flag or wearing a pin with a rainbow or the transgender flag (blue, pink, and white stripes).

We can also mind our words. Take some time to consider the words and phrases you use when talking about LGBTQ+ people and issues, especially in earshot of your grandchild. For example, if a trans person overhears a family member say something like, "There are only two genders," or, "This trans stuff is just a fad," they will be less likely to share their own personal experience or disclose to that person that they are transgender. Refining and minding your language will make it more likely that your grandchild will invite you in and share information about their identity with you.

It may take some time for you to come to a place of acceptance. One day, you may even be able to celebrate having a transgender grandchild!

For now, celebrate the fact that you have been invited in. Celebrate that your grandchild wants to share this part of themself with you and has asked you to be part of their experience. Celebrate that your grandchild has introduced you to an aspect of human variety that you didn't know much (or anything) about. Celebrate that in order to share their very personal information about their gender identity, your grandchild must have a high level of trust in you and must believe you will love them no matter what. Celebrate that they honor and respect you enough to share this deeply personal knowledge with you. Celebrate that your grandchild is living a life that is authentic and true to their deepest self. Celebrate *them*! And love them for being exactly who they are.

How Do I Tell You?

CHAYLA FISHER

(Chayla is my son Amaya's partner)

How do you tell your grandma that you are not the little girl she helped raise anymore? Your grandma who bought you the frilliest dresses she could find, who paid for your admission to an all-girl middle school, and who would ask you if you had a boyfriend almost every time she saw you as a teen? How do you tell her that you despise the fact that you are stuck in a woman's body, that the way you look—your gender—has impacted the way you've been treated your entire life and made you hate yourself? That you felt like you had to act like a certain person for your friends, family, and society to accept you?

My grandma had a Catholic upbringing in New Jersey. She married an equally Catholic man, and they raised their four kids as Catholics, even sending my mom to Catholic school (where she was picked up by her pigtails and smacked with rulers and staplers). They moved to a pretty conservative part of California and became very involved with their local church, with which my grandma is still involved. I think my grandma voted for Hillary Clinton, so perhaps I shouldn't give the impression she is entirely conservative (to be honest, politics is not something heavily discussed in our family), but I always considered her someone with a generally conservative "old school" outlook.

I remember sitting at lunch with my grandma and sister years ago. (I was a teenager at the time.) As I was snacking on some bread, somehow the conversation came around to my grandma saying, "I'm worried Hunter's gay." My cousin was about five at the time. He liked to wear a unicorn sweatshirt and princess dresses. He also demanded that I do his makeup when doing the makeup of my female cousins. I responded to my grandma with, "Well, the most important thing is that he knows you still love him no matter what." I also remember describing to her the experience that so many LGBTQ+ children go through, including being disowned by their families—and how harmful the lack of family acceptance can be, how it causes incredibly high rates of depression, suicide, and homelessness for so many LGBTQ+ kids.

This was before I was even aware of my own queer identity, when I was still stuck in the "cis-straight female" box. I didn't even know there were other options. In high school, some of my friends started to question their own sexual identities, and I continued to tell myself, "Well, you've never liked a girl, you've only been kissing them since you were in preschool, so that means you're straight and just experimenting." How do you tell yourself that this wasn't just experimenting, that kissing the daughter of your grandma's neighbor wasn't just you "being a kid"; it was you discovering your sexual and gender identity?

It wasn't until college, where I was surrounded by queer people who were so comfortable in their own identities, that I finally started to realize the many facets of my own identity. In my freshman year of college, I dated a girl for the first time, and then I met my current partner, Amaya. I went from identifying as straight to bisexual to pansexual within the course of a couple months. And a year or two later, I came out as non-binary.

I started to play around with my pronouns, quickly learning that it was difficult for most people to use *they/them*, and it felt like a hassle to ask folks to use the correct pronouns. I decided I would use *she* and *they* (interchangeably, essentially), mostly to make it easier for others who were challenged by *they*. When I came out to my dad as pansexual, he said he was, "Proud of how big my heart was." When I came out as non-binary to my mom, she asked me what it meant. She said she didn't fully understand, but that she loved me no matter what.

I remember sitting down to write a letter to my grandma to tell her I was non-binary. I had already come out on Facebook, and my mom was already trying to use my correct pronouns. I had no idea how my grandma would react. After the conversation I'd had with her about my cousin perhaps being gay, I was super anxious that she wouldn't understand. But I knew that, if my cousin *did* turn out to be gay, I would want to be the one to sit down with grandma and teach her about queer identities—and about how she can support LGBTQ+ people—so that my cousin didn't have to carry that weight on his shoulders.

I sent the letter. She wrote back a little while later, sending a brief note on a card saying that she loved me no matter what.

A couple months ago, a different cousin came out to me as queer and gender fluid/questioning. They asked me to use a different name for them, and they were elated when I told them about my gender/sexual identity. To know that I wasn't alone, that I wasn't the only "queer" in my family, made me feel elated. *We are in it together.*

On my most recent trip home (I live in another state), I learned that my grandma has been talking to other grandparents who have trans grandkids. I also learned that in the wake of the Supreme Court's *Dobbs* decision, overturning decades of protection for abortion rights, my grandma is pro-choice. She has been surprised that so many of her friends have spoken out with anti-abortion views. Who knew?!

I just recently sent a text to my grandma, suggesting she consider joining Janna's group for grandparents, a safe space where she could find community, learn, and ask questions about gender identity. I told her how much I love her and look up to her. I can only hope that she will want to continue her education, to support me and my cousin, and to be the best pro-trans grandma she can be.

Ages and Stages of Transition

There is no one way to be transgender, and there is no one trajectory that can be set for a transgender person's life. Each person is unique, and each trans person's experience is unique. Until very recently, most trans people did not transition until they were adults. Today we are seeing more and more children transition at younger and younger ages. Although there is a rapidly increasing number of resources available, there is no one guidebook or checklist all parents can follow.

Just as we describe the process of human development in stages (such as *early childhood*, *tween years*, *teenage years*, and *adulthood*), it can be said that there are certain stages a transgender person may go through on their way to living fully as their true selves. The stages of transition that I outline here may or may not match up with all trans people's experiences. Each person's experience will take its own form.

Here are the stages I noted in my son's transition:

BEFORE

Before is the time before there is any incongruence between one's assigned gender, their inner knowing of gender, or their outward expression. (For Amaya, this was from the time he was born until he was about three.)

EARLY YEARS

The *early years* describes the time when there may be some early signs of incongruence. Perhaps before the person is too young to communicate it verbally, they have an inner knowing of who they are, and they express it. For example, a two-year-old child who was assigned male at birth might insist "he" is a girl. The child might express preferences that would be stereotypically assigned to or expected of the opposite gender. Parents or others may notice the child does not behave in gender-typical ways, and people may even refer to the child as (for instance) a "tomboy" or "girly boy." Parents and others may have a feeling that the child will just grow out of it. It is in fact possible that this person *will* grow out of it, and that exploring gender is just a passing phase. Only time will tell. (For our son, this was ages three to seven.)

TWEEN YEARS

These are the years between the *early years* and *transition years*. Incongruence is present but nothing is clear. The person may or may not be aware of the incongruence. Perhaps the person now has an inner knowing, which may or may not be expressed outwardly. Or, conversely, there is some sort of outer expression of gender diversity but no inner understanding. During the *tween years*, the person may experience confusion, as may others around them (including grandparents).

The person in the *tween years* stage may begin some experimentation, perhaps "trying on" different aspects of gender expression in public or just in private—such as wearing clothing that does not conform to the stereotypical clothing choices of the gender they were assigned at birth. They may also experience isolation and frustration. There may be questions or things left unsaid (again, both by the person or by those around them). The tween, or their parents, may feel they need to reach out for support from doctors, teachers, therapists, clergy, family, or friends. (Amaya was in this stage from the time he was 7 until he was about 13.)

TRANSITION YEARS

In this stage, the person will actively affirm a gender identity that does not align with the sex they were assigned at birth. This person is purposeful in their actions and asks others to honor their requests. They may at first only tell peers, or teachers, or certain family members about their transition. In fact, it is likely they may come out in phases, perhaps taking "baby steps" at first among their most trusted inner circle of friends or loved ones. Possible incremental measures a person may undertake regarding social transition include new clothing and hair choices, a name change and/or personal pronoun change, making changes to legal identity documents, or using the bathroom or locker room of one's affirmed gender. (Amaya transitioned between the ages of 14 and 17.)

COMPLETE

To reach the *complete* stage, the person has made the adjustments necessary to live comfortably as their authentic, affirmed self. It is up to each individual to decide when their transition is complete, and this feeling of being complete may even change in the future. Some may never feel complete with their transition. (Amaya said he was "complete, for now" when he was 17.)

NOW

The current state of life. Amaya is a young adult, long past his *transition years* stage and living an authentic life as the man he was born to be.

As I mentioned before, the stages of transition do not always correspond to a person's age. Most people do not invite others in, come out, or disclose that they are questioning their gender, until at least 15, and most often in adulthood. And not everyone who has this inner realization will take steps to transition. Some may never tell a soul, while others may disclose their inner gender identity to a few people but never take any steps toward transition.

One way to think about it is that the stages above depict what we might expect for children who grow up knowing they are going to be loved, honored, respected, and accepted for whomever they may be. The more a child is exposed to and/or witnesses other people who have positive, nurtured experiences passing thorough these stages, the more likely they are to have a positive experience themselves if and when they recognize in themselves an incongruence between their assigned sex at birth and their own gender identity. Unfortunately, not all children have the benefit of feeling safe and secure enough to express their inner, true self. Others may repress those feelings or may respond to unfortunate cues in society or at home that suggest there's something wrong with them if they allow those feelings to surface.

Also, keep in mind that about a third of trans adults say they began to understand their own gender identity when they were 10 or younger.[4] This does not mean that seven-year-old children necessarily know the word *transgender*, or what it means. Rather, it means they may have an inner sense of something not being "right" with regard to their gender identity. At that age, they may be unable to express what they feel or even to give those feelings a name.

In my child's life, the stages of his transition toward living as his true self corresponded with the development stages typically used by psychologists to define childhood. For example, when Amaya was very young, before age three, he didn't express any sense of self other than what we projected onto him. These were his (and our) *before* years. Around age three, the time when humans develop the concept of a *self* that is separate from *others*, Amaya began showing us his predilection for all things boy. He was beginning to have a sense of himself and how he wanted to express his identity. These were the early years in his childhood development, and they corresponded to the *early years* on his journey of transition. When he was going through puberty, he was very much caught in the in-between. He was a girl (as we knew him then) who looked like a boy who was growing breasts. He was a tween, developmentally, and this coincided with the *tween years* of his gender journey. During his teenage years (a time of significant transition and maturation for all of us), Amaya took steps to affirm his gender, and he went through *transition*. As awkward as any teenager's experience can be, it is also typically a time of increasing independence and autonomy. After resolving his gender dysphoria during his teen years, Amaya was able to say he felt "complete, for now" at age 17.

As I said above, the stages of transition are different for everybody, and may be affected by a perception of receptivity and acceptance, social cues (positive and negative), repression or unawareness of inner feelings of gender identity, and other social and psychological factors.

Here is another example of what the ages and stages could look like for someone who transitions in adulthood. This is not based on any one person, but rather is a hypothetical combination of different experiences that have been related to me by transgender adults who transitioned in their adult years. Experiences vary widely, so this sketch is for illustrative purposes only:

Before years: Ages 0–8
Early years: Ages 8–16

Tween years: Ages 16–30
Transition years: Ages 30–35
Complete: Age 35
Now: Age 36

After they reach the *now* stage, our hypothetical trans person may have new feelings of incongruence emerge. (We are not static beings, after all.) After contemplation and therapy, this person might realize they need to take further steps to find a new congruence, and so their process could continue until they feel complete (again, for now).

Transitioning to completeness is a very personal process that is unique to each individual. There are many ways a person may change something about themself in order to find congruence, to be whole, to live as their authentic self. There are also intrinsic parts of an individual that will not change. It is important to keep this in mind, especially when one might feel they are "losing" the person they have always known. Even after transition, so much of who this person was *before* is likely to remain the same.

At this point, my grandparent readers, I'll ask you to pause and reflect:

- What steps has my grandchild taken toward living as their authentic self?
- How have I responded to these changes?
- What does my grandchild need from me right now? (Hint: *A Grand Love.*)

Part 5

WHAT *CAN* I DO?

When grandparents learn they have a transgender grandchild, or when they are asked to make changes in the way they speak about or interact with their grandchild, it can feel confusing, troubling, and daunting. There is a process to undergo for everyone in a family of a transgender person who transitions.

One grace we can offer ourselves and each other is *patience*.

Patience

(Excerpt adapted from *He's Always Been My Son*)

Patience grows out of (and feeds into) understanding. Just as all children develop a sense of self on their own unique timeline, the development of a sense of self for a child who is gender expansive or gender questioning follows its own timeline. As parents/ grandparents, we cannot force our children/grandchildren to be someone they are not. (Though many people will try, often with tragic results.) We also do not want to squelch self-expression. We must be careful not to label our children/grandchildren before they have a sense of themselves. Parents of transgender, gender-questioning, and gender-creative children must be at once actively seeking information while still practicing patience with their child's process. Grandparents who do not have the primary caregiver responsibility to take action are often left on the sidelines, watching and waiting. It can be difficult to be patient when one feels left out, confused, concerned, or fearful.

An individual's gender identity can only be understood fully from an inner place, and the development of a person's inner understanding can take time. Each person will undergo their own process. Even when our grandchildren tell us about their gender identity, it may take time for them to allow other people (even other grandparents) to know this very personal information.

A person may ask their parents to use a new name only in the presence of certain family members. They may ask for different pronouns to be used in the home—but they may want to continue to use their "old" pronouns outside the house.

Some people may ask their friends and schoolteachers to use their new names and pronouns before telling anyone in the family to start doing so. If they do so, you may feel hurt or disrespected as parents or grandparents for not being among the first wave of people asked to contribute to this part of the individual's transition. Those feelings are best kept to yourself; there's no need to add a layer of guilt to your child's/grandchild's transition experience.

It can be challenging to know how to respond in a supportive way when things change, perhaps even day to day. This is especially true for grandparents who do not live in close proximity or do not see their grandchild often.

The 2012 Trans PULSE Survey of Transgender Youth, conducted by Ontario's Trans PULSE Project (I referenced this survey earlier in Part 1), revealed that the number one factor trans youth say they feel leads to their happiness and self-acceptance is parental support. Sadly, trans and gender-expansive youth *without* family support have been shown to be in the highest risk pools for depression, anxiety, and suicide.[1] These are sobering statistics. Children (and, yes, adults too) who do not express gender in stereotypical ways need parents and grandparents who are knowledgeable, flexible, and patient.

This message is for you, grandparents: Your transgender grandchildren need YOU to support them, and to seek education and resources to develop your understanding.

It is up to you as grandparents to be one of the "adults in the room"; to take charge of your own process so you can be there to support your grandchildren. It may take a radical move on your part, and it may require you to let go of deeply held beliefs regarding both gender identity and your expectations for your grandchildren. Often, it can be helpful for grandparents to join support groups and/or seek therapy to work through their challenges and develop a sense of acceptance and peace.

Yes, grandparenting in this day and age can be surprisingly hard. But you can do this! As grandparents, you must have patience with your grandchildren, their parents (some of these are your own children, of course)—and, most of all, have patience with yourself. Keep calm and carry on! It may give you comfort to remember that you are never alone; there are always countless grandparents who feel the same and have gone through similar experiences.

The Cleft

D.W. CLARK

I discovered that my trans grandchild thought we might not love him as much as our other grandchildren because he was changing. I had a quiet talk with him to tell him about the day when he was born and we went to the hospital.

We saw him across the nursery, and he had a cleft in his chin, just like his grandfather. We were so excited, not because he was a girl or boy, we didn't care about that, but because he was part of our family, part of us, and that would never change. That was what made him special, not how he dressed or looked. We knew he would change lots over time. [When I told him about this] he didn't say much. I hugged him and left to clean up the kitchen, feeling like I had failed to make a difference.

A few minutes later I felt a tug at my shirt. This little face with the cleft in his chin then said, "Nana, love you more." Nothing else really matters, does it?

Questions and Concerns

There are some common responses, questions, and wonderings that I hear from grandparents who have learned their grandchild is transgender/non-binary or is questioning their gender.

I LOVE AND SUPPORT MY GRANDCHILD, BUT I WORRY!

It is natural for grandparents to worry about their grandchildren. Today's world gives a person good reason to have significant concerns. Trans people have historically been marginalized, "othered," and discriminated against. As I write these words today in mid-2023, there are over 500 anti-LGBTQ+ bills currently proposed in state and local legislative bodies across the U.S. Extremists and fundamentalists from many different backgrounds are inflicting harm on transgender people, especially trans youth and their families, via the media and political action, often under the guise of "protecting our children." It also seems that some politicians today scapegoat trans people for purely political, cynical, and divisive reasons. This would not be the first time in history we've seen politicians vilify "others" for the sake of votes from those in the electorate who fear people that differ in some way from those they encounter in their insular, day-to-day communities.

Unfortunately, the loudest voices in public debate are often those that sway people who are uneducated or unaware about a given topic. Thus, many people who are not exposed to current research and other information about gender (especially people who don't know any trans people themselves) all too often align themselves with ill-informed and oppressive views. This results in the stigmatization of trans people and their families, and results in legislation denying access to age-appropriate gender-affirming care. It also fosters a dangerous environment that puts trans people at risk of being the victim of hate crimes and violence.

It can be frightening for a grandparent to listen to all this hatred and anti-trans political speech and imagine it being focused on their grandchild and their family.

There are many ways to be a human.

It is deeply troubling that trans and gender-diverse people are denigrated just for being who they are.

The good news is that, despite all the negativity, there are also positive things happening. For example, there are currently (again, as of this writing) at least a dozen states, plus Washington D.C., that have passed legislation to become "safe states" for transgender youth. These states have laws now to protect the ability of transgender minors to access gender-affirming care. More states may follow suit. Grandparents can help by raising their voices, contacting their local and state legislators, and giving their time and/or money to support political action groups that fight for transgender rights. Grandparents can also help by educating their peers, work associates, and other community members.

More good news: Despite the current political climate, family members (not the government) provide some of the most significant and valuable support for trans youth. Family acceptance has been shown to greatly increase mental/emotional health and well-being for transgender children and teens, and to lower their risk of anxiety, depression, self-harm, and suicidality. In fact, a recent Trevor Project study found that having just one supportive, accepting adult in the life of a young trans person can lower their risk for suicide by 40 percent.[2]

You, my grandparent reader, could be that one person.

HOW DO I TRUST THIS IS REAL?

Sometimes it can be hard to trust that the path your grandchild is on is the right path. Perhaps thoughts of uncertainty linger in your mind—even though your heart wants to be accepting, and even though you do your best to show your love and acceptance through your actions and interactions. It's okay to feel uncertainty. As your grandchild navigates their own experiential path through transition, each person in their family and social circles (including grandparents, of course) will tread their own path toward understanding and acceptance. It's okay to exist in the unknown, as uncomfortable as it can be.

I encourage you to take time right now for some self-inquiry. Ask yourself:

- How does someone know who they are?
- How do I know who I am?

Grandparent of
a Trans Girl

GRAMMA A

I am the grandmother of a 14-year-old transgender girl whom I will refer to as "V." She is in high school. She is on puberty blockers and taking hormones. V seems happy that she can live as a girl. I am hopeful that everything will work out in life for her.

V has been very insistent on her female identity since she was very young. I remember every Halloween she'd want to be a princess or some female character. For Christmas she'd want dolls and girl toys. At the time, I had a very hard time with that. I would feel guilty for giving her a doll, like I was encouraging her to be transgender or gay. But I would continue to give her things that I knew she liked. I just felt very uncomfortable doing it.

I used to think that her parents should encourage more male activities and clothing. What I didn't know was that the parents *did* do those things. V just couldn't relate and wasn't interested in typical boy activities. She'd always choose to have a pink or purple backpack for school, and I know she was teased.

There was a period, maybe around age eight or nine, where she told us her favorite colors were now black and blue, and she got a navy-blue backpack for school, quite a switch from the girly backpacks she had previously. That didn't last very long, and she was back to pink and purple.

When she was around 11 years old, her parents made the decision, along with her, to allow her to begin presenting as female publicly. She began using a female name, and she wore dresses and girls' clothing all the time.

At around age 12, she started taking puberty blockers. And now, at age 14, she has been on hormones for at least six months. I know V went through quite a bit of therapy and counseling before she was approved for any medical intervention. I know her parents had a hard time adjusting just to having a gender non-conforming child. And now that she's been identified as transgender, they have more to worry about and plan for, especially in the unsupportive political environment in many states today.

As a grandparent, you don't get to voice your opinion on how your grandchildren are being raised and what you think their parents should or shouldn't do, unless they ask you. We have to trust that our adult children (the parents) are doing the best they can for their families. It's definitely been a journey, and one that will continue to evolve. I'm excited for V as she starts high school and this next chapter of her life.

On another note: By the time V came out as transgender, we had already been through the coming out of our own adult transgender daughter, whom I will refer to as "P." In a way, P's coming out as transgender was easier for me in the long run than V's was. I have no doubts that P is who she is, but I'm not as confident about our granddaughter V. Perhaps it's because P was an adult when she finally came out, and I see how much maturing V has left to do.

I just trust that V's parents are making the right decisions. That's the hardest part about being the grandparent.

More Questions

I LOVE AND ACCEPT MY GRANDDAUGHTER, BUT WHY DO I HAVE FEELINGS OF GRIEF?

When a person comes out as transgender, they often make changes that help them feel more aligned with their gender identity. These changes can be very important to a trans person's sense of self and wholeness, and can include changes to their name, pronouns, body, clothing/hairstyle, and more. It is notable that such changes, which can be so uplifting and affirming for the trans person, are also among the changes that most significantly elicit feelings of grief and loss for close family members.

Grandparents may grieve the loss of a chosen name given to the child as they process all the changes that gender transition brings. Names carry great value for us and may have deep significance for our family. The child may have been named at birth after a treasured relative or ancestor. Perhaps they were even named after you!

Likewise, with pronouns, there may be a profound sense of loss. Maybe you had several children, all of them boys, and your grandchild was the first and only baby girl in your bloodline. Changing to *he/him* pronouns in such a case might trigger intense feelings of sadness or other emotions.

Some grandparents may feel grief about the loss of, or the need to let go of, many of our dreams, expectations, and even perceptions of who our grandchildren are, and who we are in relation to them. (Sometimes those feelings may be unwarranted based on lingering gender stereotypes. During and after transitioning, your granddaughter may still want to shoot hoops with you on the driveway; your grandson may still want you to teach him how to sew dresses.)

From what I understand, trans people do not want people to grieve for them. They may even say grief is inappropriate or misdirected. After all, the person is not gone. They are very much alive, and they are taking steps to affirm their life. They are trying to live a life that *feels* alive to them. Often when a person transitions, they want their family to understand that the person they thought they were interacting with was not actually their authentic self. In that regard, *letting them go* (the person they seemed to be before transitioning) is more about *seeing them for who they really are* (the person they are now).

No one can or should tell anyone else how to feel. All feelings are valid. So, if you do feel grief, acknowledge it—but please don't share that feeling with your grandchild! Expressing your grief or sense of loss to your grandchild can cause them to feel hurt or make them feel that they have done something to hurt you. They may feel that they need somehow to take care of you in this moment. Instead, please *acknowledge* your own feelings to yourself and *allow* yourself to feel them. At the same time, as with all types of grief, we can get stuck sometimes. Our grieving feelings may take over; they may obscure or cloud other feelings or inhibit our growth, understanding, and acceptance. If you are feeling this way, reach out for the support of a therapist, grief counselor, support group, and/or friend. With the right approach, you can move forward from a stuck place and perhaps even let go of your feelings of grief. What you find on the other side of that grief may include acceptance, love, closer relationships, shifts in perspectives, healing, and even joy.

"When I first found out that my grandchild is transgender, I was very fearful. I did not understand. I was afraid. I didn't know what to do. After a while, after finding the support of the group, and with the help of my therapist, I decided this: I choose joy."

Grandma M

I AM HERE FOR MY GRANDCHILD. WHAT CAN I DO?

What do our trans loved ones need from us? Love. Understanding. Acceptance. Support. These are interrelated pieces of what all humans need to be happy, healthy, and whole. Where to start?

Love

You already love your grandchild (or you probably wouldn't be reading this book), and that love is a source you can draw on. Your love is, after all, *A Grand Love*. Think about what you love about your grandchild, regardless of gender. What is the special spark that is unique to that person? What does this person love to do? What do you enjoy doing together? What do you feel deep in your heart when you think about your grandchild?

Although your loved one may be in the process of changing some things about themselves in order to live as their authentic self, they are intrinsically the same grandchild you always knew. They may be going through some sort of outward-facing transformation—and because they are changing, so can you. Your love for them resides deep in your heart. Connect to that heart place and move forward from that tenderness you feel inside. You might ask yourself, "What would *love* do?"

Understanding

This can be a challenging step. It has often been said that none of us can truly understand another person, as we are each a unique, existential being. Still, the more I have in common with someone, the more I feel I can understand them (at least in part). When we are faced with something unfamiliar to us, we have a choice to remain in that unfamiliar zone and wallow in unfamiliarity, or we can seek to understand more.

I have often asked myself, "How do I as a cisgender, heterosexual woman understand the transgender experience when it is not my experience?"

When I wanted to learn more about being transgender, I sought out trans folks in my community, and also in the media, who were sharing their stories. The more I listened, the more I began to understand that being transgender is another beautiful, normal variation of being human. (I hope you are beginning to understand this by now if you've read this far!)

Grandparents of transgender grandchildren each have their own lifelong wisdom and experience to tap into. You may not have met any transgender people in your life, at least not as far as you know, before you found out your grandchild was trans. Yet, I am sure you have met many folks who have had very different life experiences from you. I'm even willing to bet that through your interactions with many different people during your lifetime so far, you have learned some things and perhaps even grown in some meaningful ways as a result of those connections.

Our grandchildren can be a source for our personal learning and growth. Sometimes, our grandchildren *want* to be people who educate others. (I certainly have encountered some fabulous young teachers!) More often than not, however, being in a position to teach others about what it means to be transgender just because a person *is* transgender can feel like a burden, especially if that person is still in the tumultuous midst of their transition. It can be very difficult for trans people to explain to others how they have an inner knowing, especially when that inner knowledge is still in the process of becoming clear to themselves.

You can develop your understanding by reading books by trans people and their family members, including my first book, *He's Always Been My Son*. When I wrote that book, there were very few stories that had been published written by parents of transgender children. In fact, there were very few positive stories about trans people published at all. Now there are a plethora of books and blogs to learn from. I encourage you to seek out these stories of courage, determination, and love. They will help you develop your understanding.

One book I highly recommend is *Before I Had the Words: On Being a Transgender Young Adult*, by author and YouTube creator Skylar Kergil.[3] Skylar gives a first-hand account about coming of age while struggling to understand his gender. He writes about the confusion he experienced and not knowing how to talk about his feelings about his gender identity. At the start of his transition, at 17, he started posting videos about his experience to YouTube. He recorded weekly videos about his physical and emotional changes that attracted thousands of followers.[4] His story is positive, encouraging, educational, and inspirational.

There are many other ways to learn. Videos, movies, documentaries, in-person events, panel presentations, and other experiences can provide insight and foster your understanding. (See the Resources at the back of the book for some suggestions.) Check out what is happening in your local libraries, LGBTQ+ centers and support organizations, and affirming places of worship in your area. Seek out examples of transgender adults living life as their authentic selves. Envision your grandchild living *their* life as their authentic self—and envision them thriving.

Consider this: Even with the best resources possible, someone who is cisgender may never truly understand what it means to be transgender. For that matter, as a cisgender woman, I am sure I will never truly understand what it means to be a man, and my cisgender husband says he is sure he will never truly understand what it means to be a woman. (And neither of us will ever truly understand what it's like to stand on top of Mount Everest, to perform open-heart surgery, or to dunk a basketball as a professional player.) Do we really need to understand another's lived experience in order to respect them? To love them?

In the absence of understanding, we can still work toward, or simply choose, acceptance.

Acceptance

Merriam-Webster defines *accepting* in this way:

> able or willing to accept something or someone; inclined to regard something or someone with acceptance rather than with hostility or fear; tending to regard different types of people and ways of life with tolerance and acceptance.[5]

Your grandchild needs your acceptance. People need to feel safe within their families and communities. Transgender people deserve to be treated with respect. It is not enough to tolerate. To tolerate is to "put up with." Tolerance is not enough. To accept is to let go of fear and hostility.

Acceptance can come through understanding. Again, in the absence of understanding, we can still work toward, or simply choose, acceptance. Connecting with and focusing on the love you have always had for your grandchild can help you move toward accepting that they are transgender or non-binary.

Attending support groups for grandparents of transgender/non-binary grandchildren can foster a greater level of acceptance. Hearing from others who also have trans grandchildren can normalize the experience and create a sense of community. It is easier to come to acceptance yourself when you know other people, including other grandparents, who are also accepting of LGBTQ+ people within their lives and communities.

The Family Acceptance Project (FAP), an initiative of San Francisco State University, distinguishes between *accepting* and *rejecting* behaviors. The FAP model provides a useful framework for understanding how these behaviors contribute to increased well-being or increased risk for LGBTQ+ youth. FAP research provides yet another confirmation that family acceptance fosters positive mental/emotional health and reduces risk for trans youth.[6]

Transgender people who are accepted by their families are less likely to be depressed, three times less likely to *attempt* suicide, three times less likely to *think about* suicide, and are significantly less likely to have substance abuse problems.[7]

Conversely, family rejection of LGBTQ+ youth has been shown to lead to higher levels of depression, suicidal thoughts, suicidal attempts, illegal drug use, and higher HIV/STD risk.[8]

Here is the Family Acceptance Project's overview of *accepting* and *rejecting* behaviors:[9]

Accepting behaviors

- Welcome your grandchild's LGBTQ+ friends to your home.
- Support your grandchild's gender expression. Participate in family support groups and activities for families with LGBTQ+ and gender-diverse children.
- Connect your grandchild with LGBTQ+ adult role models.
- Express enthusiasm for your grandchild having LGBTQ+ or gender-diverse partners when they're ready to date.
- Use your grandchild's chosen name and the pronoun that matches their gender identity.
- Require other family members to treat your grandchild with respect.
- Bring your grandchild to LGBTQ+ groups and events.
- Tell your grandchild that you're proud of them.
- Stand up for your grandchild when others mistreat them because of their LGBTQ+ identity or gender expression,

whether at home, at school, in your congregation, or in the community.

- Speak openly about your grandchild's LGBTQ+ identity, if they are out and okay with you sharing this information with others.
- Believe that your grandchild can be a happy LGBTQ+ adult and tell them that they will have a good life.
- Get accurate information to educate yourself about your grandchild's gender identity and expression.
- Show affection when your grandchild tells you or when you learn that your grandchild is LGBTQ+.

Rejecting behaviors

- Blaming your grandchild when others mistreat them because of their LGBTQ+ identity or gender expression.
- Trying to change your grandchild's LGBTQ+ identity or gender expression.
- Preventing your grandchild from having LGBTQ+ friends.
- Excluding your LGBTQ+ grandchild from family events or activities.
- Not letting your grandchild talk about their LGBTQ+ identity.
- Telling your grandchild that God will punish them because of their sexual orientation or gender identity.
- Not letting your grandchild wear clothes or hairstyles that express their gender identity.
- Making your grandchild leave the home because they are LGBTQ+.
- Calling your grandchild negative names because they are LGBTQ+ or gender diverse.
- Telling them they can pray being transgender away.
- Telling them you will pray their transness/gayness away.

- Pressuring your grandchild to be more or less masculine or feminine.

Many parents and grandparents don't mean to do harm. Rather, they may think some of the items on the *rejecting behaviors* list will actually help their trans child/grandchild fit in, avoid bullying, live a better life, and perhaps even get to Heaven. However, it bears repeating that research from FAP and many other sources tells us unequivocally that the *rejecting behaviors* above can be harmful, sometimes tragically so. It is imperative that family members understand this and learn instead to model behaviors on the *accepting behaviors* list.

Support

Support is a key protective factor for mental, emotional, and physical health and well-being for all humans. This is particularly true for transgender/non-binary youth. Just as acceptance has been documented to increase the likelihood of positive lifelong outcomes for all LGBTQ+ people, providing and enabling support for your trans grandchildren can have a significant, positive impact on their lives.

Grandparents can support their grandchildren in many ways. But due to any number of factors (including physical distance, limited or strained lines of communication with grandchildren and/or their parents, etc.) you may not be in a position where you can provide or suggest all of these ideas. And keep in mind, your grandchild may not welcome some of the suggestions for support outlined below. You also may feel you need to check in with your grandchild's parents before approaching your grandchild to offer support or provide ideas about support resources. Or you may feel it's more appropriate to advise and provide information to the parents rather than directly to your grandchild.

However, bear in mind that when parents are not accepting and supportive, grandparents often can and do fill that void. I encourage you to explore what kind of support is appropriate for your grandchild, what is possible for you to assist with or provide, and what types of support might (or might not) be welcomed. Support has many dimensions:[10]

- Emotional support
  - Sharing emotions
  - Listening
  - Expressing love, affection, care, and trust
  - Empathizing with mental/emotional health struggles
  - Finding support for yourself, such as support groups/ therapy
- Financial support
  (Note that it is imperative to avoid any type of coercion when offering financial assistance.)
  - Paying for basic needs (food, housing, health care)
  - Providing funds for transition steps such as surgery, court fees, ID document change fees
  - Contributing to educational fees
  - Helping build financial understanding and skills that lead to self-sufficiency
- Informational support
  - Researching needed information for legal/medical/ social transition
  - Vetting professionals
  - Offering advice, such as, "This is what I would do in this situation," or, "Here's what I learned, you might want to try this."
- Social and legal transition support
  - Using correct name and pronoun(s)
  - Helping with hair, clothes, makeup, nails, shaving, etc.
  - Assisting with filling out and submitting paperwork for changing ID documents, court orders
  - Finding legal representation if and when necessary

- Health care support
  - Paying for health insurance; helping with copays, deductibles, and out-of-network/uncovered costs
  - Helping to find gender-informed practitioners
  - Assisting with appointments, surgery aftercare
  - Assisting with or financing travel if care providers are not local

They Were Waiting

M.B., GRANDPARENT TO TWO
TRANSGENDER GRANDCHILDREN

When I learned my grandchildren identified as transgender, I loved them as much as ever, but I lost my way in knowing how to accommodate this change. I made their being transgender the focus of our interactions. Each time I visited, I arrived at their home with a plan of questions to ask or something relevant to tell them. For example, I looked for positive stories about transgender adults or positive trends in legislation. Many months passed before I realized this was not what they most wanted. They wanted their grandma to hang out with them, relax, be her natural goofy self, and listen deeply to whatever they wanted to share. I slowly returned to the spirit of play and attentiveness and ease in our connection. They were waiting.

A Grandmother's Perspective

GRAMMY

I became the grandparent of a transgender child two years ago. (I will call them "J" here.) The gender identity for this grandchild is "non-binary," and when I became aware this was their identity, I immediately began to research what this means. Using the correct pronouns was contrary to my strong grammatical education, but whatever it took to make them comfortable and feel loved was what I would do. I felt strongly that this child was not one to submit to peer pressure, which indicated to me that this was truly what they felt. I later learned that the self-awareness of their gender identity began to surface when J was 10, and at 14 there was a desire to address it.

Because there were four parents involved due to divorce and subsequent new marriages, I wondered if all would feel the same sense of support and acceptance. Thankfully, communication between the parents is very good, so all were on the same page in offering support. The most difficult part for me was that I was outside of the loop of information as time went on.

I had raised two wonderful people with my husband, but I quickly learned that the role of a grandparent means that one waits for information instead of prodding. The parents were all busy making plans and working through what J needed. Because of this, I engaged in my own research and discovered *He's Always Been My Son*, a wonderful book that gave me so much insight. The biggest takeaway was that everyone in the transgender person's life has his/her own concerns, thoughts, and needs in finding acceptance of the changed identity. However, the youth at the center of these situations is struggling with so many issues, so it really is not fair to use that person as one's resource for adjustment. Simple support is what is needed.

This experience in our family has caused me to feel even more strongly that the core and soul of that person is what is most important. Gender is just an external description.

This Effing Family

DOMINIC LAUREN

I have many cherished memories of childhood that involve my grandparents. When I would have sleepovers at my grandmother's house, she loved to make us mini pancakes in the morning. She taught me about the value of volunteering, working hard, laughing, and speaking up for your truth. My grandpa was someone who also loved to make other people laugh and feel good about themselves. He loved to take us on adventures and share his love for living life to the full.

While I love my grandparents, there were also times in our lives where we didn't always see eye to eye. When I came out as transgender, I was received with confusion by my grandparents. I used the word *transgender* when I was 14 to describe myself for the first time (this was in 2010). The transgender community didn't have the visibility to the extent that it does today, so there were fewer resources and less exposure to the transgender experience.

My grandparents' confusion also came from the fact that my parents didn't understand my transgender identity, so they couldn't support my grandparents in understanding who I was either. This often put me in some uncomfortable situations where family and friends mixed: my grandparents were calling me "Lauren" with *she/her* pronouns while I was being called "Dominic" with *he/him* pronouns by friends. This wasn't out of maliciousness. It came from their best understanding at the time. To them I had always been Lauren, *she*, their granddaughter. Yes, they acknowledged that I was what they described me as, a tomboy. However, they had a hard time understanding for a while that I could be a boy, or that I could be raised as a boy in a girl's body.

As a child, teen, and young adult, I would internalize these projections as my own. I remember there was a time when I first came out when I was wishing seriously to start going by the name "Dominic" instead of "Lauren." I say "seriously" because when I was in elementary school, at the age of seven, I started to go by "Dominic" with close friends as a nickname. At 14, when I would ask people to let me go by "Dominic," they wouldn't do it.

I felt like I was living a *Hannah Montana* life in some ways. (*Hannah Montana* was a television show from the early 2000s about a pop singer living a double life.) I would change clothes five times in the course of one school day because of the anxiety I felt about my gender identity. I was caught between being authentic to myself on the one hand and making my family confused and uncomfortable on the other. Now that I'm older, I know that it was never my responsibility to become their emotional caretaker, but I couldn't help feeling guilty about making people uncomfortable.

There was a period of multiple years where I never wanted to see my grandparents because I felt so uncomfortable and defeated. To me, it felt at the time like no one cared about me or cared to get to know me more. It was hard to see some family members support me while others would say that it was none of their business, that I wasn't their child and so they needed to "stay out of it." During this time, it felt like there was still an attempt by family members to maintain a relationship, but it would become polluted with the awkwardness of the unknowing.

Once I grew a little older and started taking testosterone and had top surgery, I felt empowered to talk more openly with my grandparents. I was an adult at 18, and this was the first time in my life that I was able to have legal autonomy. I felt I could finally have control of my own narrative and not fear the repercussions that existed before I attained this autonomy. I remember sitting down with my grandmother in her kitchen, the same kitchen in which she served me mini pancakes for all those years. I told her, "Grandma, you know how I have had short hair and dressed like a boy for the past four years and when I was younger? Well, I just wanted to tell you that I'm transgender. This means that I was born a girl, but I feel like a boy, and I'm going to live the rest of my life as a man."

I began to tear up when I said, "I haven't said anything to you until now because everyone else in the family told me not to tell you, because they said you wouldn't understand and that it would upset you." She looked at me with so much love in her eyes saying, "God damn it, this fucking family." Remember, she is the one who taught me to always speak my truth, ha ha.

She proceeded to say, "How come they think I'm too old to understand anything? I have known this since you were little. You always wanted to be like your older boy cousins and wear their clothes. People need to get with the times." We hugged one another, and the rest was history. She called me her grandson. She called me "Dominic." (Or a different grandson's name from time to time, for which I forgave her, because after six sons of your own and five grandsons later, I would probably mix them up too.)

Around the same time that I told my grandmother that I was transgender, I also told my grandfather. When I had a conversation with my grandpa about who I was, initially he didn't understand. He wasn't rude about it; he was actually very understanding even while voicing that it was hard for him to understand. He took his time with it and even talked to a therapist about it to further understand who I was. His process allowed for him to come to a deeper understanding of who I was as his *grandson*.

I remember sitting down with him and my aunt, with whom I was living at the time. We talked over coffee about how he finally came to an understanding of who I was. However, before this conversation happened, I didn't want to visit him. I was used to a dynamic that still felt awkward because there had been so much misunderstanding. I'm forever grateful for my aunt's encouragement to go see my grandfather because that was the first day that he started to call me "Domenico." It was a cute way for him to call me "Dominic" and affirm who I was. He gave me this nickname, and that was also the first day he called me his *grandson*.

Both of these grandparents also helped me with my top surgery in different ways. My grandpa drove me to my top surgery. My grandma also donated a little to my top surgery fundraiser to help me financially, since I had to pay for it on my own. I'm forever grateful that my grandparents came around and showed up for me in the ways that they did. Although our relationships haven't been close at times, I still love them and appreciate them for their presence in my life.

My advice to grandparents, and to any loved ones of a transgender person, is to *be aware of how your words impact your transgender loved one*. Doing a lot of research on your own to better understand your transgender loved one, instead of expecting them to educate you, is a great way to show that you care. It communicates that you are taking the time to learn.

I also have advice for other transgender individuals who might find themselves in a situation similar to mine: Remember that when members of your family don't understand who you are, it isn't a negative reflection of yourself. Although it can be hard to remember this, other people's perception of you is *their* perception, and it doesn't have to be your own. Stay open to the fact that your grandparents can learn to understand who you are, and they can be respectful of your transgender identity if given time. This requires that your grandparents also become willing to learn and grow beyond their current perception of gender.

For transgender individuals, patience is truly a virtue. The more patience you have for people, and with appropriate boundaries that you set for yourself, the more you protect yourself emotionally too. Remember to have compassion for yourself as well as others.

Part 6

TRANSITION: LOOKING FOR AND PURSUING CONGRUENCE

Transition is a life stage for transgender/gender-diverse people during which they begin to live according to their gender identity, rather than conforming to the gender that aligns with the sex they were assigned at birth. While not all transgender people transition, a great many will take at least some transitional steps at some point in their lives.

Another way to think of transition is that a person is pursuing *congruence*. As I defined in the glossary section earlier in this book, *gender congruence* is a feeling of harmony with regard to one's gender in body, mind, and heart. That is to say, congruence is an alignment of how one feels on the *inside* with regard to gender and how they feel their *outside* matches or aligns with this identity. Put another way, gender congruence means a person can express themselves outwardly in a way that aligns with their gender identity.

For most cisgender people, there is no substantial transition required to attain this alignment; we generally have been gender congruent since we were first dressed by our parents and given our first toys and haircuts. (Of course, many aspects of gender are cultural and not inherent, such as styles of dress and hair. That's a topic for another day.) Some of us may make incremental transitions at some points in our lives that are counter to stereotypical gender norms for many reasons. For instance, some cisgender men may decide they want to paint their fingernails, and some cisgender women may want to shave their heads. It is also true that gender norms shift over time. My husband points out that his mother Elaine was among the first generation of women in the U.S. to begin wearing pants. But these adaptations are, as I said, generally not a component of a substantial life stage of transition necessitated by a deep, inner sense of self and need to achieve gender congruence.

When a transgender person takes steps to transition, they are pursuing or achieving *gender congruence*.

There are several aspects or areas of life in which a person may make changes to better align themselves with their gender identity. We can categorize these transition areas as *social*, *legal*, and *medical*, and there are many different steps in each of those areas that a trans person may or may not feel is appropriate for them to take. The list below has some of the most common and critical aspects of each of these transition areas, but there are countless other steps a person may consider appropriate to achieve their unique blend of gender congruence.

SOCIAL TRANSITIONS

- Clothing
- Hairstyle
- Name
- Pronouns

LEGAL TRANSITIONS

- Court ordered name/gender marker changes
- Updating ID documents with name/gender marker including:
  - Birth certificate (most states allow this, but not all)
  - Driver's license or state ID
  - Social Security
  - Passport
- Updating all school records
- Updating medical insurance

MEDICAL TRANSITIONS

- Hormonal measures, including:
  - Puberty blockers (see note below)
  - Hormone therapy to promote physical, mental, and/or emotional alignment (again, see note below)
- Surgical measures such as the addition, removal, or modification of gender-related physical traits, including:
  - Facial feminization surgery
  - Laser hair removal
  - Phalloplasty (addition of a phallus)
  - Vaginoplasty (creation of a vagina and vulva from existing genital tissue)
  - Orchiectomy (removal of testicles)
  - Hysterectomy (removal of part or all of uterus)

This book is not intended to be a primary resource for learning about these things in depth. For more information about surgical and medical options, consider resources such as the websites for UCSF Center of Excellence for Transgender Health, UCSF Child and Adolescent Gender Center, Mount Sinai Center for Transgender

Medicine and Surgery, and the Center for Transyouth Health and Development at Children's Hospital Los Angeles.[1]

A note about puberty blockers and hormones: *puberty blockers* are used when a preadolescent trans child, their parents, and their gender-affirming medical practitioner(s) agree with due consideration that it is appropriate to prevent or stop puberty that is misaligned with the child's gender identity. Trans tweens and teens may stop using puberty blockers at some point if they determine (again, with family and medical support) they are ready to experience puberty that aligns with the sex they were assigned at birth. Others, at an appropriate age and time, will begin *hormone therapy*, which will allow them to experience puberty aligned with their identity and contribute to their gender congruence.

Hormone therapy is also an option for teens and adults who transition after puberty.

Hormone therapies include estrogen for people who identify as female and testosterone for people who identify as male. Some people may choose to begin hormone therapy because part of the gender congruence they seek is to *present* as male or female, even if they do not fall into a binary male/female inner identity. People who are non-binary, gender diverse, or otherwise don't identify specifically as only male or only female may consider a variety of options related to hormone therapy that could help them find congruence. There is no single hormone therapy solution for everyone's unique situation.

Hormone therapy is often (usually, in fact) a lifelong commitment when used for gender-affirming care. Testosterone therapy typically results in bodily changes such as increased bone and muscle mass, increased strength, facial hair growth (and an increased likelihood of male pattern baldness later in life), and deepening of the voice during puberty. Taking estrogen is likely to increase breast growth and development, reduce or eliminate facial hair growth, and decrease muscle mass and bone density.

It does not have the opposite effect on one's voice relative to testosterone.

Many transgender and gender-diverse people don't ever choose to use puberty blockers or begin hormone therapy. Others don't have access to resources and face legislative, financial, and other obstacles to receiving this kind of medical care.

This statement from Boston Children's Hospital provides some insight and current context regarding all of the medical transitions mentioned above:[2]

You may be aware that in states across the country there is a recent increase in proposed legislation aiming to restrict the rights of transgender and gender diverse youth. Many of these bills aim to restrict access to medical care and limit children and adolescents who identify as gender diverse from participation in sports.

Boston Children's Hospital has always been and always will be committed to providing the best care for ALL of our patients, regardless of their gender identity. The belief that all children deserve the opportunity to live, grow and thrive with love and support, is foundational to who we are and what we do.

At Boston Children's, we are proud to be home to the first pediatric and adolescent transgender health program in the United States, the Gender Multispecialty Service (GeMS), which has cared for more than 1,000 families to date. We believe in a gender-affirmative model of care, which supports transgender and gender diverse youth in the gender in which they identify. This is a standard of care grounded in scientific evidence, demonstrating its benefits to the health and well-being of transgender and gender diverse youth.

… We are here to affirm, uplift, and advocate for transgender and gender diverse youth, and we remain committed to doing all we can to support their care and well-being.

Again, there is no one way to be transgender. And again, not all transgender and gender non-conforming people seek medical intervention nor undergo surgery. Each person has their own needs regarding what changes they may pursue to find congruence.

As I mentioned earlier, it can also be said that as human beings, we all seek congruence with regard to our gender identity and gender expression. Our hairstyle, clothing, and mannerisms are often choices, made consciously or not, based on our gender identity and how we want to express gender. This applies to medical transitions as well. The woman who chooses breast reduction or implants, the person who has a nose job, the person who shaves their legs and armpits, and yes, even the man who uses Viagra— these are all gender-affirming choices.

When politicians and others today talk about limiting and reducing gender-affirming medical care for children and adults, they never talk about limits on gender-affirming surgeries for cisgender people. Nobody is proposing a ban on breast implants or Viagra. And yet, how are those options fundamentally different from the options that should be available to transgender people?

I mentioned earlier in this book that the need many transgender and gender-diverse people have to peel back the layers and fully reveal and affirm their truth is overpowering and compelling. The social, legal, and medical transitions they experience are often challenging, to say the least. As a grandparent, there are many paths you can take to assist and support your trans grandchild. Perhaps you are beginning to think about which of those paths are right for you.

Here is another opportunity for you to pause and reflect:

- What changes has my grandchild made, or what changes is my grandchild exploring/thinking about?
- What changes have I made, or what changes am I exploring/

thinking about in order to support my grandchild? And to support myself?

- How can I offer support and unconditional love to my grandchild as they navigate their own path, even when it seems difficult or confusing to me?

Grandma Andi's Story

Notes from a Conversation

My relationship with my grandchildren (we call them "Heart" and "Monkey") has always been positive and has been since day one. When my grandchild Heart came out at school, my daughter Sara was accepting right away. Heart came out on a Thursday, and by Monday he presented with a new name, pronouns, haircut, and clothes. Sara got him the book *I Am Jazz*, and Heart took it to school. Sara called me and my husband Ken and said, "Heart told us he's a boy." And she added, "When you are here, you can read this book."

She also said, "If you can't do that right away, don't come."

In her effort to be totally accepting and follow the child, Sara also expected others to do the same. As I was only recently informed about this, and uneducated in all things transgender, I didn't share my concern, but was fearful that things were going way too fast. My initial response was to ask if a therapist should be called, and couldn't this possibly be just a fleeting thing? At first, we did a lot of apologizing for using the wrong name or pronoun, and then we were told we don't need to apologize. Just learn. We did our best.

I remember on our first visit to Berkeley following Heart's coming out, he was participating in a cooking class with many other students. As we walked in, I kept telling myself that he was there as a boy complete with tie and apron. I needed to not make any mistakes. The registrant couldn't readily find his name on the class list. In an effort to assist, I looked up and identified him with "There she is!" It was then that I realized I still had a ways to go. I made a mental note to practice those pronouns. I so wanted to get it right. We noted on that visit that Heart had metamorphosed from a depressed little girl to a very happy boy.

Then Monkey came along: "I'm transgender too." We wondered, "Another transgender grandchild?" We were skeptical about whether she was truly transgender or just following in her sibling's footsteps. At first she declared herself transgender and was using female pronouns. Later she said she was non-binary and asked to be referred to as "they." Using *they* as singular was challenging. We cheated and used only her first name! When she later affirmed that she was a girl and asked for *she/her* pronouns, we realized that we had to catch up! On a recent visit, we noticed what a sweet girl Monkey is. She is so creative, always wanting to engage with me in the crafts that I enjoy. She wants to be helpful in every way. She is laugh-out-loud funny!

Once I asked Sara, "Why can't Heart and Monkey wear the clothes they want to wear just at home and not at school?" She answered directly: "That's how you have a child who commits suicide." It was blunt and a call to action.

We recently had a visit, the first in a very long time, and it was the best ever! Heart's voice is so deep. He has a girlfriend, and he is driving! He depicts the essence of transgender adolescent— meaning that for long time now, he has wanted to be seen, and then succeeded in seeing himself in his community as a boy, not as a *transgender* boy.

Regarding medical treatment for Heart, I believe he has the right medicine for his brain. A lot of people believe if you're transgender, you will have surgery and medical interventions. But many trans people do not do any of that due to insurance, pain, or fear of surgery, or they don't feel it's necessary, or they medically disqualify.

I live in this little town in Florida, and there are not necessarily fewer transgender people here than in Berkeley, California, where Monkey and Heart live. They just have resources and safer spaces to be open about it in Berkeley.

One thing that has been challenging about living in Florida, as opposed to the Berkeley bubble: we are surrounded by conservative Republicans. They may know gay people, but they do not know much about transgender people. I call ours a "mixed marriage," politically that is. But the one thing Ken and I are in solidarity about is how poorly trans people are treated in this country.

I was at a dinner party and overheard someone say, "If they can't make up their mind, they are an 'it' as far as I'm concerned."

That felt very hurtful. I didn't say anything at that moment, and then afterward I sent her the article from the *San Francisco Chronicle* that featured our family.[3] She later told me she was appreciative and said that she learned from it. The information was offered in a way that it could be received. She has since asked, "How is your grandson?"

I don't think there are more transgender people now, I think there are more trans people who are willing to talk about it. We are a family whose challenges along the way served to discover the best in each other.

Andy

CONNIE P

My grandson, assigned female as his gender at birth, never seemed really happy to me. Not sullen or pouty—just not truly happy. He was surprisingly competitive with his male cousins and dismissive of feminine interests and activities. That in itself didn't seem strange. Many girls and women aren't frilly and girlie. As time went on, though, I became more and more aware that Andy wasn't just a tomboy.

Thanks to the internet, he was able to research and find others like him and understand what his options were. When he was 15, he told his parents that he'd always been male, and he needed to live it. It was a very emotional time for the rest of us, but his parents stepped up, supported him, and did their own research.

It was a little easier for me to accept because I had seen it coming gradually. When I visited him or he visited me, we had lots of one-on-one time for conversations and sharing. I wasn't involved in the day-to-day life of parenting—going to work, getting kids off to school, laundry, meals. Even so, I was shocked when he made his declaration at the time that he did. I thought he'd at least wait until he was between high school and college.

And then I surprised myself. For the first time since my daughter and her husband moved over 500 miles away, nearly 20 years earlier, I was glad for the distance between us. Intellectually, I absolutely knew Andy had made a necessary and absolutely correct decision. Emotionally, I grieved for the beautiful granddaughter I had lost. I told myself that I was very lucky. At least he is still here! I felt guilty about being sad. Finally, I stopped trying to make it make sense and just allowed myself to be sorry to see *her* go.

Over the next months, it became so much easier as I watched Andy settle into his "real" life. He seemed like someone who had been released from prison—free, confident, and happy. Today I can't even remember why I was so unhappy about his perfect decision.

It's ten years later now, and Andy is a self-confident, happy young man. It's obvious that he is comfortable in his own body, and it's a joy to have watched his journey.

Unconditional Love

A Discussion with Granny

GABRIEL ADELMAN

Support from family during a transition is not only crucial, but in many cases lifesaving. In my particular case, my main support system over the last seven years of my transition has always been my Granny, Ethel Osit. While she is 68 years older than me, that has never been a barrier for our closeness.

I am very fortunate to have a grandmother who values staying educated, and Granny often refers to herself as a "lifelong student." Part of this education means that she has very progressive values, and she has always been empathetic and understanding above all else.

I spoke with her recently, and we reflected on the ways our relationship and our lives have been impacted by my transition. Spoiler alert: not that much.

I've been coming to her house for our sleepovers since I was a little kid. Even though it is now many years later and I am 21, I still visit and stay over, and we still sit and eat breakfast together in the same chairs in the same designated spots at the same table. We sat in those same chairs while I asked her a few questions I thought would provide valuable insight for anyone who may be wondering about similar things.

I began by asking her what has changed about the dynamic of our relationship during and after my transition process. She replied, "We've always been straight with each other, and we will continue to be straight with each other. I love you for who you are, not because of what your name is or what your gender is. I don't see you as different; I see you as the same person. The differences are just that, differences."

She continued: "What is different is that as you were growing up, I had visions about what you would do with your life, and that's obviously changed. But, then again, no matter what your gender is, the expectation of your parents and grandparents won't always come to fruition. The world changes, and so you have to change with the world. There's disappointments and there's surprises, good surprises, regardless of your gender."

Granny's "change with the world" philosophy is a mindset that makes her a wonderful example of how just because someone is from a different time, that doesn't mean that they can't adopt a more open-minded perspective regarding changes happening in the world around them, especially when it comes to people who they might not be used to seeing. On this topic, I asked Granny, "What are some valuable ways you feel grandparents can offer support during a close family member's transition, even if they don't completely understand yet?" She had a simple reply. "You love 'em and hug 'em and kiss 'em, no matter what they call themselves, because they are really the same person. You listen to what they say, you don't make a secret of them, and you're proud of them regardless of the circumstances. They're your babies and you love them."

For her, love is unconditional. That bond transcends any outward changes because the heart and the love inside is the same. Of course, not everything is always easy. Facing challenges along the way is very common.

I asked Granny what was difficult at the beginning of the process that became easier over time. She told me that when she told her friends I was transitioning, she expected some negative responses. But she was surprised when nobody had an issue at all. She stressed the importance of overcoming the fear of what others might think and instead focusing on the love you have for your grandchild.

I asked if she had any final words of wisdom for anybody wondering how to best support a transgender loved one, or anyone going through something challenging. She said, "It's important to have some source of comfort and trust in somebody that you know has your interests at heart, and they don't have an axe to grind. It's your security blanket."

For me, when life was too much to handle, spending time with her made me feel safe and comfortable. It may sound simple, but the most valuable thing you can offer to a person in your life as a grandparent is to let them know they are loved, and to be proud of them. Creating a space where that transgender person can feel loved and safe to express themselves authentically can strengthen the love and bond you already have with each other. You don't have to "get it" right away, but creating a relationship where that person feels unconditionally embraced can make all the difference.

My Interview
with Carol

Sometimes grandparents are needed to be the main caregiver and support for their grandchild. I'll introduce you now to Carol. Carol is a psychologist and grandmother to her only grandchild, a grandson who is transgender. We sat down together recently for an interview.

Carol: I'm a grandparent—but, for various reasons, I've been in the role of not so much *parent*, but as a caretaker and social worker. I help him, my grandson. You know, everything he has done is important for him to do. I have always been very involved in his life, but he didn't live with me until he was 18. Now he's 22. I think we have gotten a lot of work done together on his journey. One of the things that happened was that he found The Spahr Center, which is just a fabulous organization and really has helped him a lot.

When my grandson, granddaughter at the time, was around 12 or 13, he was going through puberty. That is when he told us he was a boy, he was a man. He described it this way: he put on men's, boys' clothes, and he just knew that was right for him.

When he was little, he (she at the time) would wear a lot of boys' clothes. He really did. If he had to wear a skirt or a dress, he would put tights on underneath it, and we thought he was a "tomboy." I remember thinking in the back of my head, "Hmm, you know, maybe—"

Janna: Might you have been doing some gender questioning of your own about your grandchild?

Carol: Right, I mean, just the extent to which he resisted anything feminine, especially clothes. He was never into cars, typical boys' kinds of things, or dolls. He was very artistic and kind of androgynous with his playthings.

When he was very little, I remember he had pants and a vest and a tie. But, you know, I think I just didn't want it to be true because I didn't want to have all that difficulty in life for him. So, I was always kind of pushing him to wear dresses. At his cousins' *b'nai mitzvah*, he was 12, he wore a dress. But underneath, he had, you know, tights—not even tights, but more like slacks, pants.

It was when he went through puberty that it really became an issue for him. He and I had the struggles over clothes, and I have since apologized to him about it. I said, "I really didn't know; you hadn't told me." I had a sense, but I was hoping that it wasn't going to turn out that way. He wasn't clear enough. I will never know exactly, but I think probably he was not ready to tell me. I think that he did have the feeling for a long time.

Janna: I want to ask about what you said, about hoping that it wasn't true. I think a lot of people have that experience, so I think it's worthy of exploration. Please tell me more about that. Why do you think you had those feelings?

Carol: I think it was because my family had a lot of special needs. It can be hard on a family and on the person, so at first, it felt like, "Wow, now we have this to deal with."

Janna: So perhaps this felt like one more cause for concern about your grandchild. At the time did you know much about transgender people, did you have any experience?

Carol: No, not much. When I was in graduate school, we had a class that was part of the program for the doctorate I got in family therapy. It was called "Alternative Lifestyles," and the teacher brought in a whole bunch of people, and they talked to us. They were gay, or they were polyamorous, the gamut. There was one trans male who spoke to us, and that was the first time I had any kind of exposure. I remember him talking about his surgeries. Now that we are looking at things, I note the advances that have been made. That was back in the 80s.

Janna: It sounds like you had a little bit of understanding, you knew that trans people existed, but you hadn't had a personal experience.

When I read the book *Before I Had The Words,* by Skylar Kergil, the title and concept strongly resonated with me. What do you think about that idea with regard to your grandchild?

Carol: Yes, I think so. I have never really had any conversation in depth about how he began to understand and how much he knew. I think it wasn't until he went through puberty that the feelings were so strong. He was probably afraid to talk about them, until it became absolutely imperative for him.

Janna: What do you feel helped you "get it," to know that you needed to be that fierce grandma that would "go to the mat" for your grandson?

Carol: It didn't feel like a decision, you know what I mean? [At this point, she was tearing up.] I have always had incredibly deep feelings for him. He is my only grandchild, and before I even knew [about his gender], I was always on his side, very protective.

Janna: What do you think is important for grandparents of transgender grandchildren to know?

Carol: What comes to mind is that there's nothing wrong with them. It's just a difference, a diversity. *There is nothing wrong with them.* As a grandparent, you can be worried or sad and wish they didn't have to go through what they have to go through, but you cannot pretend it doesn't exist.

Our understanding as grandparents—you know, we are from the dark ages. We gotta get with it.

You can't be fixated on the past, with all of your ideas of how things could be. People of my generation, we have to keep changing. It's not just about our trans kids, it's about everything. We have to keep changing.

Listen to your grandchild and let your grandchild tell you what's true for them. You might think, "Maybe this is a phase"—well, maybe it is, but you are not going to say that. You are going to say, "Tell me more, tell me more about that, tell me about your experience, tell me about your feelings, tell me what you are thinking." Do not impose your own ideas on them. Give them room. And if they say something, believe them, respect it.

Janna: What are some of the gifts? We talk about the challenges, but I think it is important to focus on the joys or gifts or insights that come from this experience in a positive way.

Carol: It makes me cry to think about it. Joyful. Poignant. A hard journey. It's when he is happy, that's the gift.

That is everything to me.

When he got his blue belt in karate, he was so anxious about it. When he has these victories, I am beyond thrilled.

It's like you would do with any child or grandchild. You would want to give them all the tools they need to be successful. There might be more to do, more to overcome, and yet you can make a tremendous difference. I would say to grandparents, you're really, really important.

* * *

Grandparents make a difference in the here and now—and in many ways, even after they have left this Earth. While you, and all grandparents, may have deep feelings of fear and uncertainty, it is also true that you, and every grandparent, have a choice regarding how you will *respond* at each moment in the life of your grandchildren. Certainly, this is true regarding support and acceptance of gender. When grandparents love and affirm their grandchildren for who they authentically are, it is an act of love. Yes, love is a feeling—but love is also an act, an expression, a behavior. Acts of love that are consistently supportive and accepting become a legacy of love.

How do you want to be remembered? What are you doing to meet this moment and every moment with the kind of love your grandchild needs and deserves? I have an answer; you will meet every moment with *A Grand Love*.

To Doug, Sue, and Robert

JASPER LAUTER

I need to tell you something
And you're allowed to take all the time you need
I'm a boy
That's right
I'm a man

I am no longer the little girl running through the sand
If you've seen me through the years this probably doesn't come
as much of a surprise
Throwing tantrums, wearing dresses
Putting up with all the lies

Take a second to think about what this means to you
Maybe you want to throw a bible at me
Maybe you want to shut me out
Maybe you're just happy to have a grandson
But I'm still me

Same flower
Different box
Finally growing in the right garden
I know you will still love me
You don't have to understand
But you do have to respect me

It is not easy
Flipping your idea of me on its head
But I am finally comfortable being honest with you
And I want you to be able to enjoy my authenticity as much as
I do

The Only Grandmother I Knew

WHESTON CHANCELLOR GROVE

An introductory note from Janna: Grandparents can also be people who are not related by blood. Still, their love and presence in one's life can be deeply impactful.

* * *

My grandmother didn't like her first name. She went by her middle name, LaVerne. She found me and my older sister through a program my mom had looked into after hearing about it at our private Catholic elementary school. It was designed specifically for matching individuals with families seeking surrogate elders. My mother and father didn't want us growing up without grandparents. All of my biological grandparents died before I was born or soon after. I was told my paternal grandmother held me as a newborn. She died a month or two later. LaVerne was the only grandmother I ever knew. The fact that she wasn't blood related made no difference. She loved us and we loved her.

She lived in an upscale mobile home park for seniors in Sunnyvale, California. She had two very successful children, a son and daughter. She was an avid traveler who collected teddy bears. At Christmas we'd go to her house and bake cookies from scratch. Kneading the dough with flour, we'd flatten it to a pancake with a giant rolling pin, then we'd use different-shaped cookie cutters before adding sprinkles. After that, into the oven they went.

As a child, the process seemed to take hours. While the cookies baked, my sister and I would select a Disney VHS to watch. My grandma had them all. I always enjoyed *Lady and the Tramp*. I wanted to be the Tramp because of his carefree way of enjoying life. I relished the opening scene where he awakes in a barrel at the railroad tracks, steam whistle for alarm clock, he stretches and rinses off under a leaking pipe. Blue skies and a happy-go-lucky stride. The Tramp didn't require anything except wide open spaces. He felt hemmed in by social norms.

At Easter, we dyed eggs. We always had two hunts. One at home—I grew up in an 1888 Victorian on one of the longest streets in San Jose—and a second egg hunt at our grandma's. I remember the orange trees running alongside my grandmother's porch, redolent of citrus, and the white rocks. The soft sound of her front door, opening onto a room with her washer and dryer, made her home feel insulated. Carport and house were lightweight in texture, seemingly aluminum, reminiscent of the durable material I imagined space shuttles to be made of—muffled, safe, designed to weather any condition.

My Grandma LaVerne came from an era of grit, born between the two world wars. She worked in a lab with radiation, in what capacity I can't say. What I do know is she lived to be just shy of 97. Obviously, she had been well protected from the radiation.

After my parents divorced, we moved east to Virginia, and I saw my grandma less and less. She came to visit for my 14th birthday, when I still looked much as I ever had. Skinny as a bean pole, brown hair past my shoulders, breasts starting to rise, no telltale signs of distress to the casual observer. I didn't realize what was wrong for another year. There were inklings, but I did not know about the medical condition called gender dysphoria.

My mother took me to a slew of therapists and, on one or two occasions, to a PFLAG group in an effort to get information. I seldom spoke in these circumstances. I was taciturn and resented going. Can a parent's love be *too* unconditional? Concerned, she sought resources and supported me the only way she knew how. More than anything, she wanted to alleviate my suffering. She accepted me no matter what and would literally walk through fire for her children.

LaVerne flew in for my sister's graduation from the College of William and Mary four years later. I wore a belt and pants, clearly masculine. If my grandma had any suspicions about my gender incongruency or sexual orientation, she made no show of it. A year later, in June 2003, she returned for my graduation from high school. For 12 months up to that point, I'd worn my hair as short as a boy's, having cut it the summer before my senior year.

I had also legally changed my name in November 2002. Much to my anger, the teacher in charge of my high school's yearbook included the wrong name. Not once, but three times. What made the situation inexcusable was the fact that I had been on the year-book staff—in her class!—so she well knew about the situation. I'd been going by *Wheston* throughout my senior year. Having the wrong name printed in the yearbook was mortifying. I will never forget going to pick up my yearbook, excited to see the finished product, and flipping to the layout of seniors' portrait pictures. Everything in me froze. *How could she?* Students in my classes who knew nothing about my gender confronted me in a curious manner. I felt exposed. Harrison, a kid in my keyboarding class, came right up to me and asked, "Did you see? It says you're—" he was keen to know. My teacher, Mr. Allister, was listening, monitoring in case he might need to intervene. I brushed the matter aside. "They got it wrong, misprinted it." "Yeah, but three times," Harrison pursued.

It means nothing to me now—all the black-and-white faces in

all the yearbooks buried in so many closets, all forgotten. What hurt and devastated my adolescent perspective was the knowledge that the yearbook teacher's actions had been deliberate. No one could be so innocently negligent. The wrong name had been used not once, not twice, but *three* times in the book! I wanted to be remembered correctly by peers and teachers. A printed name lives on forever. One day, one of those many classmates who has the yearbook tucked in a box in a closet will pull it out and flip through the senior pictures. I'll be remembered because my picture is awkward. The name exists as the only proof of who I had been for 17 years.

The afternoon that I picked up the yearbook and told my mother, she marched inside the school to speak with the teacher who had presided over its production. I regret not confronting her myself or going in with my mother. I was too upset, too young and reserved to voice my contempt. The teacher expressed her apologies to my mother. The fact remains, however, that in the last few days of the school year, the teacher never made any gesture to apologize to me. She could have written a note or found me somewhere on campus and said how sorry she was to my face. Neither my mom nor I believed she was sorry. If it was a mistake, how "out to lunch" could she have been? In the end, she should have said something directly to me. She chose not to and that says enough.

On graduation day I donned the male ceremonial robe. All the boys had black caps and gowns; the girls wore green. When they called my name, the speaker announced "Wheston Chancellor Grove," and I strode across the stage for all to witness. Flatchested, bound tightly. When the commencement concluded, students threw their mortarboards into the air. They dropped like downed birds. I wish I could have erupted in similar elation. In contrast, I gently removed my square hat, wanting to ensure I kept the tassel. My emotions proved conflicted. Glad to be seen and announced as male in front of my peers and former teachers,

I was equally melancholic, sad that four years were gone and I could never reclaim them. I wasn't ready to be an adult in the social realm. I wanted to be a 12-year-old boy for a while and experience male adolescence.

My Grandma LaVerne gave me a card and a present with the name *Wheston* scrolled on the front. She always had the most legible handwriting. The inside of the card said something along the lines of "Happy Graduation, Grandson." Not once did I ever detect a hint of dismay, not a word or glance, regarding my transition. I do not know how my mother told her, in what context—through letter or phone call—but being long distance served as a buffer. If my grandma thought my becoming male was outrageous or unnatural, I will never know. But I never sensed it. My grandma looked the same in my eyes for 20 years. Short, penciled-on eyebrows, bespectacled, and curly red-brown hair, tightly cropped. My coming out as trans seemed unceremonious where she was concerned.

Did she detect the tightness in my face, the redness around my eyes, from violently crying the afternoon right after my graduation? I'd returned home and gone upstairs to my mother's bedroom to be alone. I had no friends. My family would be going out to dinner that night at The Whaling Company—all of us. I was inconsolable. My mother came up and found me. Through choking convulsions, I said, "I'm tired of living." I was 18, going to college in a few months, and without hope. Young, blinded by depression, I was unable to see the boundless possibilities. I had no social foothold. I was uncomfortable in my skin and continued to bind my chest with duct tape. I hated the female orbs. I'd yet to undergo gender reassignment surgery.

I asked my mother not to tell anyone downstairs (my sister, my dad who had flown in from California, and my grandma) that I was a sobbing basket case upstairs. "Tell me what I can do?" she asked.

"Nothing," I replied.

"Just come down when you're ready," and she let me be.

A void had spread through me. Socially, sexually, and emotionally I wasn't prepared for life. From 9th through 12th grade, I'd lived a solitary existence, excelling academically and graduating with a 3.9 average. I did not have a single friend. No recreation. Uncomfortable in my body, I'd stopped engaging in sports after 8th grade. I rarely spoke in school. I ate lunch alone every single day, observing everyone. I attended the literary magazine club, forcing myself to read poems of lamentation, longing, and spiritual death to other oddball members. At night, I'd turn the light off and steal onto my front porch, listening to the change of seasons. I was paralyzed in my skin, aching to be free.

Did my grandma know I'd been crying that afternoon? What did she think of my short hair and the blue tie with Wile E. Coyotes around my neck? Maybe she thought *this is just life*, or *I'm only here for a few days, be gracious*—or maybe, truly, she didn't care because she'd signed up to be my grandmother all those years ago.

Grandma LaVerne had a persevering temperament. She told me she'd once seen Amelia Earhart speak. She had outlived her first husband and remarried. Her second husband, Sandy, gave me my first fishing pole and tackle box for my ninth or tenth birthday. We went fishing several times. My grandma survived the death of her son to a grueling battle with prostate cancer. He was in his fifties. When her friends died, and in the case of her son, she always took to volunteering in the hospital gift shop. She kept busy, pushed forward somehow, some way. In her 90s, she traveled through Western Europe, often on her daughter's boat. For several years, she resided in France.

The last time I saw my Grandma LaVerne was in 2009. I flew to California to visit my father, and I made it a point to see my grandma as well. Years passed after that. Card exchanges dwindled, which tends to happen as grandchildren cease to be young adults. She was overseas so much with her daughter that contact became difficult. At 51, her daughter gave birth to a son, my grandma's first biological grandchild.

I never had a chance to say goodbye. All I have are memories. The many board games we played together. Yahtzee was a favorite. I still see my grandma with her word search puzzle books. She always took one with her to pass the time. She'd look at her watch frequently, out of habit. A punctual woman. I admired her tenacity and grit.

There are moments when all the years come rushing back. The weight of loneliness, like a blue whale, pushes down—a megalith shadow obscuring the sunlight. I swim and swim. Even when I manage to surface, the whale dives deeper and its wake pulls me down. Hormones have not been fun. Losing my hair has not made me feel great. What happened to that happy kid watching *Lady and the Tramp* with his sister, waiting for cookies to rise and cool on a carefree December afternoon?

I try not to think about my discontent. Not many people know my story. I do not enjoy being a hybrid gender. I feel like I live on the backside of a lie. I always wanted to be male. But even with hormones and surgery, I will never be male. It's biologically impossible. (Despite transitioning 20 years ago, there are physical traits that reveal my biological sex. That's neither a positive nor a negative statement. For me, it's just a fact.) Thus, I reside in the no-man's land of sex. I'm a third gender. Sometimes I'm sad. Sometimes I'm grateful. Other days I surrender. Mostly, I'm world-weary. I think of my Grandma LaVerne, her perseverance and affection. She will never know I've written this. I wish I could share it with her! If I live a few more decades, maybe like her I'll volunteer for an adopt-a-grandchild program.

* * *

Note from Janna: Human lives are linear in that we are born, we live, we die. Still, for most of us, our lives unfold along a path that does not feel linear. There are many twists and turns and obstacles. For some of us—not just people who are transgender—the feeling of being able to live as our authentic selves feels unreachable. Our path can seem convoluted or impossible to navigate. Still, each human is deserving of love. When a person's love is offered unconditionally, that love can be a comfort on our journey, a light in the dark that helps us see the way forward, and a means to overcoming the obstacles we encounter on our path. For trans youth in particular, grandparents and grandparent figures can provide that comfort, that light, the means to overcome impediments. Indeed, such love is *A Grand Love*.

Part 7

FIND SUPPORT
FOR YOURSELF

As I said earlier, when someone in a family takes steps to find congruence with regard to their gender, to *transition*, each person in the family also goes through their own transition. All family members will have to adjust in some way to whatever changes their family member is making. There may be a new name, new pronouns, changes to hairstyle or clothing, changes to participation in certain activities, and more. Each of these changes may have a different type and level of impact on each family member. Also, remember that each transgender person will have their own timeline and process on the way toward finding congruence—and so too will family members have their own timeline and process on the way to acceptance and integration.

In some instances, a grandchild may even transition fully (perhaps they are already "complete, for now") before one or more grandparents even become aware there is anything going on. In particular, grandparents who live far from their grandkids, and/ or who are not in frequent contact with them for any number of reasons, may find out all at once about several incremental gender-related changes. It's a lot to adjust to at once!

Unfortunately, some family members may "adjust" to another family member's gender-related transition by declaring themselves unwilling to change or to accept other people's changes. They may even "adjust" by shutting loved ones out completely. But I trust if you've read this far, dear grandparent, you do not want to be one of those people.

Some of the challenges related to family member adjustments are unique to the type of relationship a person has with their trans family member. Here is a list of some challenges that may resonate with grandparents in particular.

TRANSITION CHALLENGES FOR GRANDPARENTS

- Expectations vs. reality
- Community norms and values
- Religious beliefs
- Political ideologies
- Distance
- Perceived loss of what "was"
- Cognitive challenges

Can you think of anything else? What are your challenges?

It is important to recognize these challenges and then to find the support you need so you can be fully present in your grandchild's life. When you do receive support, you will be able to better support your grandchild—and also to support *your* child, the trans child's parent, and their spouse/partner.

When thinking of how to go about getting this support, the Circles of Support model can be helpful. Employing this model, the person at the center would get the support they need from the circles surrounding them. Each surrounding circle offers support facing inward, so to speak, while seeking outward from their circle for their own support.

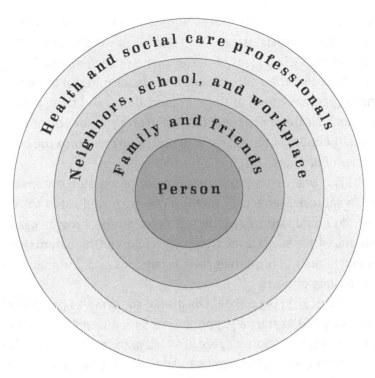

Circles of Support

For example, let's consider a transgender person in the center vantage point. This person looks for support from the circles surrounding them. First, they turn to *family and friends*. Those folks can provide support for the person at the center of the model, to the trans person. To receive their own support, *family and friends* can look to the surrounding circle of *neighbors, school, and workplace*, and beyond that circle to *health and social care professionals*. *family and friends* may also find support from community groups and places of worship, among other places, which may fall into either of the two latter circles. Likewise, the trans person in the middle has (theoretically) access to support from those outer circles as well.

When grandparents need support, they may be inclined to seek it from their grandchildren: "Explain this to me." "But, how do you know?" They may also seek support from their own children, the parents of their grandchild: "What if this is a phase?" "How will I adjust?" While some of the recipients of such questions may be able to offer their support and provide meaningful responses, many (perhaps most) of those grandchildren and their parents will not have the energy or the ability to give you the answers you need. It behoves grandparents to seek guidance from the outer Circles of Support.

This is where community and support/discussion groups can be so valuable, especially when the group is dedicated to supporting grandparents specifically. These groups provide grandparents with a space away from their children (the parents) and grandchildren to have their own discussions and find their own community of peers.

In fall of 2020 (again, this was during the Covid-19 pandemic), I was inspired to start a support/discussion group for grandparents. I wanted to create a space in which grandparents could find information, build community, and develop a sense of belonging during that unique and challenging time. One grandparent was so moved by the idea that she decided to donate the needed funds to our local LGBTQ+ organization in Marin County, The Spahr Center, and the group was launched!

Recently, I asked some of the members of the group to comment on their experiences. These are some of the responses. (I am sharing most of these anonymously, but all of these grandparents gave their permission for me to publish these comments.)

WHY DID YOU JOIN A SUPPORT GROUP FOR GRANDPARENTS OF TRANSGENDER GRANDCHILDREN? HOW HAVE YOU BENEFITED FROM THIS GROUP?

"I think that it is important to not just say you are supportive of your child or grandchild. You have to be supportive. I didn't know how to find a group at first. I Googled it. I was more drawn to this group after I had sat in on a different one, it was more like a lecture. We didn't feel we could learn from that. We only see them [our grandchild] three times a year. We don't get to practice. We wanted to figure out a way to show that support."

"Originally, I joined the group because I was miserable. I was told my grandchild was transgender. I was ashamed. I didn't want to tell any of my friends. I had so many questions, I did not understand. The group has been a lifesaver. I have become comfortable and can share experiences with my grandson. I got better as he got better."

"I just have to say, this is a wonderful group. In our family, it's been a while, we've been through the hard stuff. I see how people change—see them so lost, and then you get it, we're right in there together."

"Thank you for giving me the tools to help our grandson through his journey. I so look forward to seeing our other grandparents [in these group sessions]. I feel as though they have become my extended family, hearing the same concerns, knowing that our family are not alone."

"Whether you feel you need it or not, you need it. Listening to other people, kindness is offered and received."

"The reason we started—first of all, our daughter suggested it. We were having trouble with the pronouns. She told us about the group, and we heard about it from another friend. Realized we knew absolutely nothing about what a transgender person goes through. Not just trans. Many others who do not describe themselves as cis. People want to be loved and safe. They are authentic, real people. Not people who are making stuff up. They truly know how they feel. We want to give him the respect he deserves as a person."

"If I hadn't come here and listened to everyone's experience, I wouldn't know kids six years old feel this way."

"To be here with others that we can be open with, there is understanding."

"I need tools, I need to know how to talk about it."

"This group helped me, helped my grandchild, helped us embrace. The group has come at a good time in my life. I found myself thinking this morning, 'Oh good, we are going to meet!'"

"My role is support, acceptance, and love."

"This group is so affirming and helpful."

"Education is very important. They are people. This is a human being."

"I love our Zoom meeting. I consider you and all the grandparents my extended family."

"We as a group have become a village of caring and supportive grandparents."

I also received some longer responses to my group query that are worth sharing in their entirety on the following pages.

My T

GRAMMA E

At the age of 13, our grandchild shared his newfound understanding of his gender with us. Or better put, he "let us in." I prefer this rather than "coming out" because it reminds me it is a privilege to be part of his journey and that he loves and trusts us.

T and his family lived 2000 miles away. He and I have always had a close, healthy, and loving relationship regardless of the geographical distance that separates us. Still, my mind was filled with concerns. How would this change our relationship? Would I need to lock up and throw away the key to precious memories with T before his transition?

Looking back, I recognize it was a bit dramatic on my part. Fear can do that to a person. Transgender and what it means to be transgender was, and still is, new territory for our family. I've learned to try my best and, when I stumble, to extend grace to myself.

T is the same T I have loved since birth. T is changing as all teenagers do, regardless of gender.

Four years later, our family continues this journey together. Watching and really listening to T has taught me so much. The grandparents' support group facilitated by Janna has been instrumental. Through this group, I have gained a wealth of information, made friendships that are precious, and have a resource to turn to. We lift one another up, we laugh together, we cry sometimes, but most of all it reminds me I am not alone in my questions, concerns, and love for my grandchild.

Here is my new and improved perspective...my learning curve needs to grow with *all* people, and who better to start with than those I love the most. It is not their responsibility to change to align with my opinions or beliefs. It is mine, to come alongside and say, "I love you, I support you, and I affirm your right to choose."

Pride Ride

JACKIE C

After joining The Spahr Center's grandparents' support group that was available on Zoom, it was such a relief to be able to talk with others about our grandkid's transitions and to feel comfortable and not alone.

Our group was represented by folks from all over the country, and only a few of us were from the local Bay Area. It was a pleasure when one of the other local grandmothers asked if I'd like to meet for coffee and a walk one afternoon. We had a good laugh the day we met and discovered that neither of us drank coffee in the afternoon! Zoom is such a blessing, but there's nothing like getting to meet in person.

A few months later, we met again during Pride Month. She suggested we meet to caravan from one community to the other to see the places that supported our LGBTQ+ people by flying the Pride flag for the month of June. It was a very hot day, and even though we got lost a couple of times, we still had a fun time. The happiness we felt to see the city halls and schools that were willing to offer support to the grandchildren we so dearly love meant so much to us.

It is hard to really capture what a great day that was!

I'm so grateful to The Spahr Center for the support they offer to the Marin County community.

Reflections on My Grandchild's Journey from Girl at Birth to Boy at Age 15

DIDI DAVIS

I can look back now and see that I instinctively knew my grand-child was not at all interested in being seen and known as the girl she was born as, even though I spent many years trying to ignore it. Mostly, I told myself it was because I didn't want her life to be harder than it had to be while growing up, not wanting her to suffer the stigma of being gay in current American culture, not wanting her to have challenges finding friends and feeling accepted. Now, with age, I see that my excuses were focused on what I thought and felt, which means of course I wasn't really thinking about how she thought and felt.

The little things I saw that instinctively told me she didn't fit the girly mode were things such as her choosing to always play the "knight in shining armor," not the "princess in distress," in playtime from about the age of five or six. Or the way she always wanted to play with the boys, not the girls, from as early as four years old. Or the way that the girls in her kindergarten class would go play as a group but exclude her. And the boys would be doing their boy things, and she wouldn't know quite where or how to fit in. (I helped out at her school for several years, so I got to watch all this firsthand.)

Later, at about age seven, she no longer liked the girls' shoes or dresses I bought her, and at eight she refused to wear girls' bathing suits, choosing instead something that really covered her body, like swim trunks and a tee shirt. These are observations I share in hopes that other parents and grandparents will recognize them and perhaps save their kids/grandkids from being unseen or unheard for who they really are, even if it doesn't fit what we want for them!

Forward to preteen years, and though I knew this transgender journey was already happening for my grandchild, it still bugged me to the core that she didn't try to dress or fix herself or her hair up like the other girls, and in so doing didn't fit in with the boys at school either. But at that age, sexuality [gender] begins asserting itself, so the boys really hung only with each other. Now, she did have a couple of very close boy friends who have stayed close friends up to today, so it wasn't as isolating as if there hadn't been any close kid friends who also happened to be males. But preteen and teen angst is so raw that it made me deeply sad to see this ongoing struggle in her life. We turned to horses for fun, and, of course, an animal doesn't discriminate about gender, they discriminate about authenticity and love. So we had many good years working with horses and other horse kids, along with various sports which were character building as well.

The point, though, is that I am sorry now that in my confusion and unwillingness to trust what I already knew about my grandchild's internal struggle, that I may have made life harder for my grandchild just because of my being judgmental—of my grandchild's life choice, clothing choices, etc. That's the part I hope other parents and grandparents can really examine in their own hearts and avoid if at all possible.

Finally, in the present day, after a year of identifying as *they*, my grandchild now identifies as *he*, even though he hasn't changed his name from a distinctly feminine one. That's difficult for me when introducing him to friends who don't get the reason why we call him "he" when his name is still the same, which many might consider a female name. It makes it harder for those people, but I don't care, I just explain it by saying he will change names when he's ready!

Recently, he spent a week visiting us, which was super because it brought home to me that this is the very same person whom I have loved all my life, and who is just as sweet and kind as ever inside. He still gives some of the best hugs I've ever known, just very innocent and loving even while traversing such difficult ground. I pray the journey forward is as easy, safe, and life-affirming as possible, and no matter what, I'll always love him with my whole forever grandmother's heart!

Part 8

FROM COMPASSION TO ACTION

Grandparents as Allies and Advocates

This part of the book is about supporting trans rights and equality in our families and in our communities.

Earlier in this book, I shared my mother's letter to my dearly departed father about her grandson Amaya (my son). Here are some more words of wisdom from my mother, Linda Masia:

> "I've learned so much on this journey with Amaya and family. I think it has helped me have a good influence on my local group of friends. Everyone in the group has grandchildren.
>
> A couple of these grandmas have had surprises as their grandchildren have chosen to 'let them in.' One grandchild shared that she is gay and another that she is non-binary. These grandmas are loving and accepting and practicing pronouns as necessary.
>
> Now there are no secrets, there is love and acceptance, and sometimes this statement can be heard: 'I don't understand it, but I love that kid!'"

Did you notice any common threads in these thoughts, or among the comments I shared earlier from the grandparents in my group? Or perhaps you recognize some of your own thoughts in their words? For some of those grandparents, it took a while to develop the understanding required to move toward their grandchild and to recognize what their grandchild needed from them. It isn't that they questioned their love for their grandchild; rather, they were confused, they needed time. They needed to find support for themselves (sometimes in our group, sometimes elsewhere) so they could move beyond whatever challenges or blocks were in the way in order to fully embrace their grandchild, regardless of gender.

Here is a pattern I have observed over the years I have been doing this work.

At first, many grandparents come into the support/discussion groups I facilitate feeling nervous, doubting "this" is real, or hoping "this" isn't true. They are worried about everything, fearful of what their grandchild will have to go through. They worry about their own children, the parents of their grandchild. Sometimes they worry about what others will think of them and their family. They are often confused and scared, and sometimes they are slow to accept, let alone embrace, their grandchild's gender identity.

But then, in our support/discussion group setting, grandparents find community. They see they are not alone. They have the opportunity to be with others who are experiencing a similar journey, others who have transgender grandchildren. There is so much wisdom and compassion in these groups. As the grandparents in my groups learn about what it means to be transgender, and as they get the support they need, most do come to accept and even celebrate their grandchild's authentic expression of self.

Oh yes, they still worry. Parents and grandparents, we worry! It's part of the job. But grandparents who seek and find support, who educate themselves and each other, and who allow themselves to grow and adapt—these grandparents are able to be the person their grandchild needs them to be. They are loving, supportive, and present for their trans grandchildren, and sometimes they become the greatest ally and advocate those grandchildren have.

As I noted earlier, much research confirms that it just takes one person in the life of a transgender person who fully accepts and affirms them to greatly increase their sense of well-being and reduce their risk of self-harm and suicidality.[1] What kind of love could be more grand than that?

As grandparents adjust to the new norm in their own families and become better equipped to affirm and support their own family member, some broaden their view to greater acceptance of, and advocacy for, the wider LGBTQ+ community. Often, this is a community whose needs were not necessarily something grandparents had paid much attention to, or did not take into much consideration, prior to their own experience with their trans grandchildren. Some grandparents find they are more apt to speak up when someone speaks disparagingly of LGBTQ+ people in their earshot, or makes an inappropriate joke, or expresses an opinion that suggests they are uninformed about what it means to be LGBTQ+ in today's world.

A Conversation with Grampy Jerry

I had the chance to talk with Jerry recently. Jerry is the grandfather, "Grampy," of a transgender grandchild.

We met initially at a local town's annual summer festival parade. Parade participants include local school staff members and students, floats with rock and roll bands and other musicians, some classic car owners showing off their wheels, and a wide variety of other community participants. The Spahr Center participates in the parade to provide a Pride contingent. Our marchers include lots of LGBTQ+ people as well as family members and other allies, people of all ages. We were colorful, with lots of rainbows and lots of pink, blue, and white, the colors of the transgender flag.

This is a town known for its hippie lifestyle, and as I have been known to say on occasion, "When the queers and the hippies get together, you know there's gonna be love and rainbows."

Jerry had a different take on it. It was his first time joining The Spahr Center for any event, and he admitted he was a little on edge. He later told me, "I know that there's assholes in this town, and I felt very much on guard." He said that he used to be prone to physical responses, a fighter, but he told me he now uses what he referred to as his "mental and verbal aikido." He said, "I was not comfortable [during the parade]. I was comfortable being a grandparent of a trans person, but I really can't let my guard down. I feel very protective of all my family and people who I love."

Jerry went on: "I consider myself hetero. I've always been bored with someone's preoccupation with someone else's sexuality or gender." Speaking generally, he said, "What you do is your own business and none of mine."

I asked Jerry to talk about how he felt when he first found out about his grandchild's gender identity.

"I really wasn't fazed all that much. I adore this child. I don't relate the way some people do. I don't treat him any differently. I still call him 'sweetheart.' I think we have a very close relationship, grandfather to grandson. A lot of men detach from their grandchild or children. I've never become emotionally unattached. We have a really strong bond."

"On the one hand, it's kind of a challenging, deep subject. On the other hand, it is no big deal."

Jerry added, "I am aware of transphobia and homophobia, and I fear for the kids. I feel protective toward all kids and adults as well."

He was very frank with me and admitted there are times and places when he is not sure he wants to wear his pride on the outside. For example, if he's going to a barbecue, he might consider wearing a T-shirt declaring he is the "Proud grandparent of a transgender grandchild." But he admits that he might not wear that same shirt in certain situations, especially where he thinks someone might say something inappropriate.

He said this is why he has to practice his "mental aikido" and remember that he has a choice in how to respond: "If you go to a friend's barbecue, and you know someone is going to be there, someone who is going to make trouble, you can decide what you are going to do. And if you don't want to engage, you don't have to. You can just walk away. You can even run away."

Jerry makes an important point here: even those of us who are fierce allies are still allowed and encouraged to make good choices about where, when, and how we will speak up. We can ask ourselves, "Is this someone I would want to get into this discussion with? And do I want to do that at this moment? And what would my grandchild want?" This doesn't mean we *never* engage; it just means we don't *have* to.

Jerry ended with this: "All the transgender people I've seen, they're all different. There's a wide array of who these people are, all human beings."

Upstanders

Jerry can be described as an *upstander.* Upstanders are people who speak up for others in the face of negativity, hate, or discrimination. They are people who typically might not bring up or engage in dialogue about politics or similar "controversial" topics in conversation with others. Some upstanders do not tend to speak their minds at all, especially when others have a lot to say. But these upstander grandparents understand that we are not merely talking about politics, we are talking about *human lives*. Transgender people are humans, and they deserve the same rights as all humans—equal rights under the law as well as social and other rights. They deserve to be accepted for being who they are.

These are some thoughts I have collected from grandparents who have expanded their own understanding of LGBTQ+ concerns and want to do something to make the world a better and safer place for humans of all varieties. They are great examples of upstanders.

"My latest concern was sparked while watching a Rachel Maddow program that was devoted to LGBTQ+ rights, and she was discussing the horrific notions some political

people have about transgender issues. I am concerned what transgender youth feel from this. This is prejudice."

Grandma M

"I have also discussed [transgender issues] with friends in the PTSD [post-traumatic stress disorder] group I am in."

Grandpa G

"It amazes me that after all these years, people still get it wrong. My friends know. They've had lunch with my grandson. He is my grandson. Still, they misgender him and use the wrong pronoun. I don't stand for it. I say, 'Even after all this time? C'mon. You have to get it right.'"

Grandma L

"My generation really disappoints me sometimes."

Grandma J

The concern these grandparents and many others feel is deep enough that they speak up, even when it doesn't come easy to them. They speak up in spaces where people may not be as well-informed about, nor personally connected to, transgender people. They speak up to inform and educate people who are unaware and/or unconcerned about the violence and discrimination that is being waged upon trans youth and adults.

I asked some of these grandparents to describe how they might respond when someone says something off-putting, ignorant, or outright disparaging. Perhaps grandparents reading these examples will be inspired to respond similarly.

"Say nothing. Silence is golden. Not responding discourages further conversations. Not anger or animosity. It is very grounded. Just say nothing."

Grandma M

"Have realistic expectations."

Grandpa J

"Make it personal: 'You are talking about my family member.'"

Grandma L

"This is a very personal thing. If it was my story, it would be easier. This is not mine, it's my grandchild's. I don't really volunteer that information [about my grandchild being transgender]. I might speak in more general terms rather than relating my response to my grandchild."

Grandma Y

"Respond with a sandwich:

Start with one 'slice of bread': 'I am so happy to be with you right now. Our friendship is so important to me.' Add the 'meat': 'This conversation is making me uncomfortable, and I want to maximize the time I have with you.' End with another 'slice of bread': 'I love you.' Or, 'I respect you and hope you can respect where I am coming from.'"

Grandma E

Turning their compassion into action, upstander grandparents can and do make a difference in the fight for equality and social justice for trans and other gender-diverse people.

I'll introduce you now to Jeanne Vargas, who turned her compassion for her son, Will (whose story you read earlier in this book), into action.

My Will

JEANNE VARGAS, GRANDMOTHER TO WILL VARGAS

On January 19, 2019, our grandchild arranged time to talk with my wife Kelly and me.

Kelly and I have been together for 21 years and married for 14 years. We got married in 2008, when it was legal in California. I came out in my early 30s, not really knowing or allowing myself to consider being with a woman. I was a single parent with a 12-year-old son. It was very difficult to deal with my own feelings about being a lesbian, let alone my son's feelings and my family's feelings at this time.

I kept it a secret for many years from my parents and some of my siblings. I did not know how to deal with it. Once I'd shared my story with my family, life became easier within my family, but it was still such a secret in my outside world. I think now that maybe I was so ready to help Will because I knew what it was like holding a secret and not living your true authentic self.

Now, getting back to our talk with Will: I knew this meeting was going to be intense. Thoughts went through my head that maybe they wanted to talk about how they'd made the varsity basketball team, or they'd started their period. Will always presented himself as more masculine, and I always thought he was going towards the lesbian life.

No, I was wrong. Our grandchild—who I will refer to with his new name, Will, and his new pronouns, *he/him*—shared his innermost secret with us about how he felt in his body.

We sat down to talk on the couch with one gender, and then after our talk, we got up with another.

That day turned my world upside down. I was shocked, but not by the fact that he revealed who he was, but by how we did not know how to help him, especially in a world that I was not knowledgeable about. I realized Will had been thinking about this for a long time. He had watched YouTube videos with teachings of the trans world. He was preparing himself as well as he could be in this new life that he now possesses. I had a lot to learn.

My wife Kelly, Will's other grandmother, was well-versed in this world, being a physician's assistant in the LGBTQ+ community. She was not as surprised as me. With her medical background, she knew what was in store, and again from a medical background, she was grounded.

My mind was going through all the negatives I have seen, such as the world not accepting him, family not accepting him, suicide rates. I wondered, "How is he going to manage this? He is 14 years old. How does he really feel? Is he strong enough to handle the world being a transgender male?"

Then I got to work. After he told his parents, Will's mom shared a book with me that her coworker had got for her. When she'd told her coworker about Will, he went across the street from where they worked and purchased a book they had on the shelf, *He's Always Been My Son*. Well, I read it—and then immediately called Janna, who was nice enough to take my call and get an earful of my thoughts and questions. Janna was my personal savior; her book was my bible.

It was then I found out what resources were available in our area. The closest was about 18 miles away. ("Over the hill," as we call it where I live on the "coastside.") I was in a hurry to get him to a transgender informative gathering, and we took him to this one at the San Mateo County Pride Center. After walking him in, my wife and I left him there. We went to a bar, had a drink, and worried.

Well, I did take him over the hill, and it was one of the worst nights of his life. They were having a talk about transgender sex, and he was about to just die. Oh, this was not a good move on our part. He was not ready for that. I would recommend that you do more research on topics before sending a child into a group such as this.

Shortly thereafter, an idea went off in my head about bringing resources to where we live here on the coast. That is when, along this path, ideas started to align. All the while, I was opening up Janna's story and saying to myself, "Thank you, Janna, for walking this path before us and giving us guidance." Like I said, it was my bible, and believe you me, I think I referred to it more than 100 times.

Then I met with someone who is now one of my favorite people, Ryan Fouts from Outlet (an LGBTQ+ youth center) in Redwood City. Ryan helped us along our path. He helped with my vision and asked me straight out, "What do you see?" As I sat in his office, I thought, "I want *this* in Half Moon Bay. I want the San Mateo County Pride Center in Half Moon Bay on our coastside."

I then reached out to people along my path who would be a significant piece of this organization/puzzle. People I did not know, but I saw their photo on a local magazine, a part of the LGBTQ+ community, parents very involved with the school with a gender-fluid child. On Facebook, I connected with an accountant who might be interested in doing pro bono work with us, a woman who I remembered had started a Rainbow Woman's Club on the coast. I knew she would be interested. And then, in February, on the front page of the *Half Moon Bay Review*, there was an article on LGBTQ+ people in San Mateo County with information about how LGBTQ+ is represented here on the coast. And it was not good news. It was then that I contacted Jenny Walter, who was on the board of San Mateo LGBTQ+ Commission. We met at our local coffee shop.

A few months after that, in May of 2019, CoastPride was created on the coastside, serving communities from Pescadero to Pacifica.

Meanwhile, we were struggling to understand Will's life challenges and, at the same time, support his mother, father, and brother—it was not easy. Everyone was understanding, but we were learning as we went. We were a great support team, but that does not mean it was easy. I was always thinking, "Is Will okay? How can we make his life easier, and meanwhile deal with our own feelings?" I personally was so occupied with thinking about Will, and I was always asking him questions: "How are you doing?" "What do you think about this?" "How was your day at school?" "What are you doing to fill your days?" "How can we help you?" Oh, my goodness, poor guy. Thank goodness he felt the love, but it was hard to watch him go dark sometimes with gender dysphoria.

There were struggles at school with pronouns, misgendering, bathroom use, and wrong names being used after officially changed. To be called your dead name in a classroom in front of others has got to be one of the hardest situations to get through. The school system is working on that not happening, but when it does it's like a stab in the heart. I have done it several times myself; even after years, all of a sudden, his dead name pops up for some odd reason. When it does, I feel terrible, and I apologize and move on.

Will has determination. He knew who he is and what he wanted. We know Will very well, as we are a close family. We knew when he wanted top surgery that we would push to get it. His mother was a huge advocate for him, an advocate to get things done in a timely manner as Will needed. Will is a lucky guy to have the father he has, another huge supporter. He would drop everything for his sons. As I look back, I am so proud of Justin and Darci (Will's parents) for stepping up and joining Will where he was on his path, and for joining the CoastPride caregiver support group to help the family on this journey.

His brother Kaden, oh—I am blessed with two big-hearted grandsons. Kaden and Will are very tight. Not that they are like the perfect siblings and don't get in each other's face, but they love each other so much. When Will told his brother about himself, Kaden's reaction was, *Wow, how lucky are you to be both genders in one lifetime!* There were many times that Kaden was in the shadows, but we all tried to really be attentive to this, because we are all human, we all need love and kindness. He got a little lost in the shuffle, but I believe we were all open and made up for it by addressing it as the journey continued. There is no perfect upbringing, that is the beauty of love and support. We deal with life as we go, with an open heart and openness to forgiveness.

There is so much more to tell and share, but I must say, we are a blessed family. We all love each other despite our differences. We support each other and feel grateful to have each other in our lives, and the support of many others in our community. My prayer for the LGBTQ+ community and allies is that they feel supported and loved, and that everyone will get to live as their authentic selves in this lifetime.

At the time of writing this story, Will is in college. He is doing well, he is also working, and he has a love in his life.

CoastPride is into its fourth year now and continues to serve our community, with many people on board who are dedicated to making the coastside an LGBTQ+-friendly region.

* * *

Note from Janna: Jeanne's story moves me tremendously. I am humbled that she refers to me as an inspiration, a spark. The story I shared, the story of me and my son, Amaya, and our family, was perhaps a spark that ignited the fuel that had already amassed inside Jeanne. But the way I see it, it was Will, her grandchild, who was the fuel. Will was the impetus for CoastPride.

Jeanne was, of course, primarily inspired by her own experiences as the grandmother of a transgender grandchild. She was inspired not only to directly support and affirm him, but also to create a new organization that would not only benefit her own grandchild, but also the entire community. From one to many, Jeanne's efforts created a legacy of love in her community. Jeanne was an upstander, and her work has inspired and enabled others to become upstanders.

Grandparents initially may not consider they have anything to offer to others outside their immediate family, or even to other family members. It takes a lot for some people just to support their trans grandchild—they may not have the impetus, time, or energy to be advocates for anyone else. Still, many grandparents find small but meaningful ways to contribute to the broader community of trans youth and other LGBTQ+ people by assisting and supporting the efforts of active advocates, educators, counselors, and gender-related supporters. Those who offered me the use of their words in this book are part of a wide and vital network of support and advocacy. They too are upstanders.

Lifelong Learners

One thing all the grandparents featured in this book have in common is that they are lifelong learners.

Lifelong learners are people who can learn and grow and expand their ways of thinking and being in the world. They can take the wisdom and knowledge they have gained throughout their lives and apply it to new experiences, and even offer it to new generations. But they do not limit themselves to what they already know. Lifelong learners stay updated, take in new information, and adapt their way of being in the present world accordingly.

What follows is a piece that exemplifies lifelong learning. It was written by Amaya's paternal grandmother, my husband's mother Elaine. Grandma Elaine died in February of 2023, not long before the completion of this book. Our family misses her greatly. Elaine was truly a lifelong learner and was in many ways a woman ahead of her time.

For my first book, Elaine wrote a wonderful essay called "My Amaya" that included this musing:

What might seem to be a set of confusing statements expresses an enrichment of sexual-gender identification, all referring to Amaya's relationship to me and vice versa:

- She is my youngest grandchild.

- He is my youngest grandchild.
- She is my youngest granddaughter.
- He is my youngest granddaughter.
- She is my youngest grandson.
- He is my youngest grandson, or transgrandson.

Of course, I worry about physical and physiological issues. I never imagined that a grandchild of mine would opt for a double mastectomy at 16! But I think it was a mature decision. He has comrades and is rather calm when facing the confusion of strangers. I do suppose I wish Amaya would change his first name or add a name to it, but that's my problem and none of my business.

Elaine spent the last 18 months of her life living in an assisted living community. Always the educator and truly a lifelong learner, Elaine had shared her insights and wonderings about gender and gender identity with some of the folks at the assisted living center where she lived, including the activities director. This director was inspired by Elaine, and he became interested in the topic of gender diversity as a result. He invited me to deliver a presentation for the residents about understanding gender identity and supporting transgender loved ones and community members. Elaine brought all her friends to my talk, and there was quite a good turnout. Their questions and comments were sensitive, insightful, and thought provoking. Her influence now lives on in the folks with whom she shared this part of her life.

My Amaya, Parts 2–6

ELAINE BARKIN, AMAYA'S PATERNAL GRANDMOTHER

POSTSCRIPT: MY AMAYA 2

December 2015

It has been more than a year since I wrote the words above [in the previous chapter]. Amaya is now preparing to go to college in Portland, Oregon, a milieu he says is congenial to the LGBTQ+ community. Now post double mastectomy, now taking testosterone, Amaya's voice has deepened, his chest is flat—and as I wrote above, he has remained the same person but not the same person. That's the odd rub. More self-assured, as independent as always, valuing his privacy and yet perhaps a tad more sociable. And the pronoun shift has become easier for me.

2014 and 2015 have been the years of T-consciousness-raising! Pundits and politicians and POTUS have all referred to trans people in public commentaries. Documentaries, books, and websites are available for those who want to learn more. A spate of midlife adults and seniors have come out publicly. All of which, we hope, has been good for Amaya and the rest of us. Confusion, negativity, and nastiness will remain among various individuals and entire nations. But Amaya has a lot to look forward to, and I am confident he will live a full, productive, and fantastic life.

POST-POSTSCRIPT: MY AMAYA 3
June 13, 2016

Today is one day after the horror in Orlando[2] and five days after Amaya's graduation from Nova Independent Study High School in Novato. George and I flew up, Burbank to Oakland, to be at his graduation and to spend time with family: Amaya, his dad Gabriel (our no. 3 son), Amaya's mom Janna, sister Emily, maternal grandma Linda Masia, and Jesse, his uncle (our no. 2 son). The contrast between the two events cannot be starker—the graduation an outpouring of love and acceptance; Orlando an embodiment of hate and malevolence. For many days after Orlando, the lyrics of Oscar Hammerstein II's "You've Got to Be Carefully Taught" from *South Pacific* (which I'd seen 67 years ago) ran through my head, something about how we are taught to be afraid of people with different eyes and skin shade.

The graduation was special in many ways: a relatively small group—ca. 60 graduates, about 20 in Amaya's indie program and 40 in Marin Oaks High School. The group comprised a Crayola-like array of flesh-tones, from pale pinks—aka "white," definitely in the minority at this graduation—through various ochres, siennas, and umbers, and encompassing a wide age range. Several teachers took turns speaking personally and directly to each student as they mounted the steps to receive their degrees, with yowling, clapping, and stomping—from folks in chairs on the floors and benches in the bleachers—accompanying each graduate. Amaya's shiny royal blue gown was bedecked with medals: the principal's award for academic achievement; for being a Renaissance Man (the latter my favorite); an Honors award and two scholarships from the Rotary Club ($$$$!).

Afterwards we went out for dinner, and all were very proud! Amaya looks wonderful, a handsome 18+ year old with loads of friends. He now stands fully up straight, smiles a lot, and is so obviously more comfortable with himself and the rest of the world, and is himself a supportive person. At dinner that night, all was so much more comfortable, and the annoyance I experienced years back when waiters said to Amaya, *And what will you have, young man?* was gone. Now, young manhood is what Amaya is in the midst of and will be for a bunch of years to come.

Whether the Orlando killer was motivated by a dedication to ISIS or an act of homophobia doesn't matter; it was probably a combination of both with a mix of self-hatred. That it happened around the time of the annual nationwide Pride celebrations has only increased awareness, for better and for worse, of LGBTQs, their presence, and their legal problems. I write "for worse" because such "publicity" is rarely beneficial for a minority population, in this instance maybe ca. 2.5 percent of Americans. But Amaya, I write again, has love, support, and many friends of all stripes!

Amaya will be going to Portland State University in Oregon (and is probably there as you read this), currently planning to major in clinical psychology and enrolled in a cohort freshman year program. Portland is said to be a congenial city for the LGBTQ+ community, for vegans, masseurs, and yoga teachers, for flower adults, yuppies, hippies, and housing developers who are gentrifying like crazy.

So again, with down deep wishes for a future marked by love (which is not "all you need," but always a boon), inclusivity, intelligence, goodwill, a caring community, and enjoyment of life and life's work.

PPPS: MY AMAYA 4
June 30, 2016

Today, June 30, the U.S. military has decided to allow transgender men and women to serve openly in all of the armed forces, another notch in the transgender belt, so to speak, although I hope that Amaya will never want or have to serve. Moreover, in recent primaries for Congress (Colorado) and the Senate (Utah), two openly transgender women, both Progressive Democrats, have won and will run against Republican incumbents in November. Misty Plowright in Colorado and Misty K. Snow in Utah! Politics may not be in Amaya's future but so much is possible these days. Ya never know.

PPPPS: MY AMAYA 5

December 16, 2016

My final comment, written after Amaya's first semester, which ended with the peaceful protest in the streets of Portland after the results of the 2016 election, Amaya's first time as a participant in the American election process. He will have much to protest against and to be in favor of supporting. We are all so very proud of him and his ever-evolving development as a caring, intelligent, thoughtful person, looking for and defining his own way in a knotty world.

PPPPPS: AMAYA 6

July 2022

The past three years have been the worst in my long lifetime in almost every respect: socially, culturally, politically, family-wise, stability, environmentally, mentally, physically, and if I have not exhausted all possibilities and categories, feel free to add them. My life has been topsy-turvied: George, my dear husband, father, grandfather, great-grandfather, uncle died in December 2020. Jesse's new teaching appointment (as of late 2019) led him to Wuhan where, as you know, Covid-19 hit the news in January of 2020. In August of 2021, I was, unwillingly, removed from my home of 47 years to a senior retirement-assisted living place in San Rafael, California, near my youngest son and his wife, parents of Amaya.

Amaya, however, has in many senses thrived during these years. After graduation from Portland State University in Portland, Oregon, Amaya and his partner, Chayla, found an affordable apartment. Both are employed and work from home. Last year, Freddie, their beloved dog, joined the family.

Meanwhile, many in Congress, the Senate, and especially the U.S. Supreme Court have been doing their best to vilify a small percentage of the American population; doing their best to deny rights of citizenship, the right to love and marry whom they wish, the right to be known by others as they know themselves. A lot of hogwash about such and such not being in the Constitution, hence not deserving of protection, has been expressed by a powerful minority of racist, phobic, self-righteous, hypocritical men and women who have the power to destroy the lives of many U.S. citizens. DISGUSTING, SHAMEFUL. SHAMELESS.

Amaya, rather discreetly, goes about his life and his business as would any or most 25-year-olds. Recently he visited me; as usual we enjoyed one another's company. He took me for a drive through a nearby redwood forest. He drives quite well, but more to the point, he is driving a now-17-year-old Subaru Legacy, still in reasonably good shape, low mileage since its previous owner (my husband George) stopped driving in 2020, a bit scratched yet comfortable.

My difficulty with pronouns for Amaya has abated. However, new pronoun issues have arisen, which I totally grasp intellectually and socially but which remain close to impossible to adopt. I get it: pan-gender, gender, bi-, non-gender individuals, neither he nor she, regard themselves as *they*.

I've read articles about gender-neutral ways of speaking, about adding the words *both* and *neither* on applications or licenses, and that since 2014 the new meaning of "they" has been added in the latest edition of the *Oxford English Dictionary*.[3] Overcoming more than 80 years of speaking English in a learned grammatical pattern stymies me. Basically, none of this has anything to do with Amaya, but it's part of the new milieu for us all.

On the other hand, Amaya's concerns about gender are not the sole focus of his life, and that's as I believe it should be. He is who he has become, or maybe that should be: he has become who he is. One of my smart, good-looking, fun-to-be-with grandchildren, my youngest grandson. However, he is subject to far more scrutiny, social and legislative rulings, prejudice, and disinformation than my other three grandsons.

* * *

Note from Janna: Elaine did not feel this piece was finished. She confided in me several times that using *they/them* pronouns was very difficult for her, and she said didn't want to wax on about that as she didn't want to belabor the point. I am sure that, in time, she would have adjusted.

When she wanted to be, Elaine was a great connector with people, wanting to know more about the folks with whom she interacted, including those who cared for her in her final years. I remember the joy she expressed when she recounted a story about a visit from people from Guide Dogs for the Blind who visited the center where she lived. She noted that one of the dogs had a rainbow collar, which she recognized as being Pride flag colors. She felt moved to show the human companion the Pride rainbow socks she was wearing. The person flashed a big smile, in turn showing Elaine her rainbow bandana. They made a connection, heart to heart.

She was a great grandma. Hers was *A Grand Love.*

Conclusion: What Is *A Grand Love*?

When I was brainstorming a title for this book, I turned to my family for ideas. My daughter Emily said, "How about 'A Grand Love?'" I knew immediately, from the feeling in my heart and the goosebumps on my arms, that *A Grand Love* was indeed the title of this book.

A Grand Love is ultimately a story born from love, a story of compassion in action. Loving a grandchild is indeed *A Grand Love*. And that love is exactly and especially vital for any grandchild who is transgender.

If you are the grandparent of a transgender or gender-diverse child, ask yourself:

- What is my goal for my relationship with my grandchild?
- What does it mean to have a "good" relationship with my grandchild?
- Do I desire to be close to this grandchild?
- Do I intend to love and support my grandchild to be the best, authentic version of themselves they can be?
- How can I show my love?
- What is the legacy I want to leave?

If your goal is to love, support, and accept your grandchild for who they authentically are, then I encourage you to consider what actions and choices will bring you closer to your grandchild. If you have made it here to the end of this book, I believe it is safe to say that you might very well consider yourself a lifelong learner who is capable of *A Grand Love*.

This brings us to the end of this collection of stories. But, rest assured, this most certainly is not the end of *A Grand Love*. Love is not some imaginary concept or mere feeling. Love is compassion in action. Love can be a compass that guides us towards empathy and understanding. Love urges us to extend kindness without expectation.

As the grandparent of a transgender grandchild, what does *A Grand Love* mean to you?

* * *

I'll end with a reminder of my top five tips for grandparents of transgender grandchildren:

1. **Be Love.** Love your grandchild. All children deserve to be loved unconditionally. (Yes, this bears repeating.) It is a sure sign your grandchild trusts you if they tell you something deeply personal, such as when they invite you into their experience by telling you, "I'm trans."
2. **Be Approachable.** Regardless of your grandchild's gender identity, remind them that you are there for them. You might say, "You can tell me anything. You can text me, send me an email. You can draw a picture. You can talk to me in whatever way works for you. And you don't have to do any of that, and still, I am here." Respond in a way that keeps the door open.
3. **Be Patient.** Have patience with your grandchild—and with yourself. Your grandchild is probably many steps ahead

of you. They probably have been thinking about this for much longer than you know. It's okay for you to take time to process this new information and learn more about it.

4. **Be Curious.** Keep an open mind. It's okay to not know the answers. You can ask your grandchild, "Can you tell me more about that?" Or ask them, "How do you feel about that?" Sometimes they don't want to be asked. That's okay too. If you sense (or if they tell you) that's the case, find someone you *can* ask.

5. **Be Supported.** Seek out knowledgeable, gender-informed, affirming support. There are numerous online support groups for family members of transgender people, including some groups specifically for grandparents. You might even find there is an in-person support group in your area. Ask a trusted friend to help you find resources. Find a good therapist or a mentor to help you tread this new path. There is a wealth of information available online and elsewhere to help you along.

And finally, dear grandparent, please consider the words of Gramma E, offered earlier in this book:

> *"We grandparents are a blanket of love covering all LGBTQ+ grandchildren across the nation."*

We all have stories to tell. Through sharing our stories, we can give voice to the voiceless. Now you are invited in, invited to weave your own story into that blanket of love, and invited to share your love, which is certainly *A Grand Love*.

RESOURCES

This is a list of some of my favorite resources. There are many more sources available, and I encourage you to reach out to one of the organizations on the list below if you want to find something in your area.

Please visit my website: www.hesalwaysbeenmyson.com to find out more about the groups I facilitate, coaching with me, events, resources, and more.

NATIONAL SUPPORT RESOURCES IN THE U.S.
Gender Spectrum
National organization providing information, resources and education for transgender youth and families.

www.genderspectrum.org

PFLAG
National organization dedicated to supporting, educating, and advocating for LGBTQ+ people and those who love them.

https://pflag.org

Stand With Trans

A national organization founded by the mother of a trans child, providing support, education, and resources for trans youth and their loved ones.

https://standwithtrans.org

Ally Parents

A group of parents of transgender children who provide direct support to trans and non-binary youth and adult caregivers.

https://standwithtrans.org/ally-parents

DOROT

Information and online programming (including my group for grandparents of trans children) to combat and alleviate isolation and loneliness for older adults and build social connections.

https://dorotusa.org

Transgender Law Center

Legal services, resources (including assistance with IDs and legal documentation), and helpline provided by the largest national trans-led organization.

http://transgenderlawcenter.org

National Center for Transgender Equality

The U.S.'s leading social justice advocacy organization providing services for trans people (including assistance with legal documents and anti-discrimination issues).

http://transequality.org

Southern Poverty Law Center

Social justice organization monitoring hate groups and working to remove barriers to equality for LGBTQ+ people and other marginalized groups.

www.splcenter.org/issues/lgbtq-rights

Trans Families

Support for transgender and gender-diverse children providing programs for youth and family members.

https://transfamilies.org

Real Mama Bears

An organization dedicated to supporting, educating, and empowering families with LGBTQ+ members through private groups, programs, and resources.

http://realmamabears.org

Trans Families Support Services

Support organization that provides training, assistance for trans people in need of medical and other types of insurance, and other programs for trans youth and families.

www.transfamilysos.org

The Trevor Project

Focused on suicide prevention efforts for LGBTQ+ youth, including a crises line and extensive, helpful data and research.

www.thetrevorproject.org/section/resources

Trans Student Educational Resources

A youth-led organization dedicated to transforming the educational environment for trans and gender non-conforming students through advocacy and empowerment.

www.transstudent.org

Camp Aranu'tiq / Harbor Camps

Organization dedicated to building confidence, resilience, and community for transgender and non-binary youth and their families through camp experiences.

https://harborcamps.org

San Francisco Bay Area resources

I live in this area, so I am particularly familiar with the resources listed below. The organizations above can help you find similar resources in your area.

UCSF Center of Excellence for Transgender Health

Offers comprehensive medical and psychological care as well as significant research, advocacy, and legal support for transgender and non-binary children and adolescents.

http://transhealth.ucsf.edu

CoastPride

A community organization in Half Moon Bay that offers a safe space online and at community events to gather the diversity of our voices, raise awareness of LGBTQ issues, and address the needs of our LGBTQ youth, families, and adults.

https://coastpride.org

Pacific Center

The oldest LGBTQ+ center in the Bay Area, provides a sliding scale mental health clinic for LGBTQ+ people, including therapy, peer-to-peer support groups, and facilitated workshops.

www.pacificcenter.org

Camp Indigo
(open to all U.S. residents)

Summer day camp for trans and gender-diverse youth.

www.thecampindigo.org

Outlandish

Organization that addresses the unique mental health challenges faced by LGBTQ+ adolescents and transitional youth and promotes resilience, empowerment, and self-acceptance.

www.queerlifespace.org/youth-services

Trans Heartline

A safe, affordable non-profit, post-op recovery house for trans individuals to stay while healing after gender-affirmation surgery.

https://transheartline.org

Suicide prevention hotlines
988 Suicide & Crisis Lifeline

CALL 988
https://988lifeline.org

Crisis Text Line

TEXT 741741
www.crisistextline.org

The Trevor Project

866-488-7386

www.thetrevorproject.org

Trans Lifeline

877-565-8860

www.translifeline.org

NATIONAL SUPPORT RESOURCES IN THE U.K.

National Health Service (NHS)

Download this guide for parents looking for support:

www.nhs.uk/nhs-services/how-to-find-an-nhs-gender-identity-clinic

U.K. non-profit organizations

UK Trans Info

UK Trans Info is a nationwide charity focused on improving the lives of transgender and non-binary people in the UK.

https://uktransinfo.org

The Gender Trust

The Gender Trust is a listening ear, a caring support network, and an information centre for anyone with any question or problem concerning their gender identity, or whose loved one is struggling with gender identity issues.

http://gendertrust.org.uk

Press for Change

Press for Change has been a key lobbying and legal support organization for trans people in the UK since its formation in 1992.

www.pfc.org.uk

Gendered Intelligence

Gendered Intelligence is a trans-led charity which aims to increase understanding of gender diversity and improve the lives of trans people.

http://genderedintelligence.co.uk

BLOGS

These are blogs written by transgender people:

www.alokvmenon.com/blog
https://genderqueer.me
https://cassiebrighter.com

These blogs are written by parents of transgender children:

https://callhimhunter.wordpress.com
www.hesalwaysbeenmyson.com/blog

BOOKS

These two books really helped me understand my child:

The Transgender Child by Stephanie Brill (Cleis Press, updated edition, 2020)
Gender Born, Gender Made by Diane Ehrensaft (The Experiment, 2011)

These are also very helpful:

The Transgender Teen by Stephanie Brill and Lisa Kenney (Cleis Press, 2016)

The Gender Creative Child by Diane Ehrensaft (The Experiment, 2016)

The Reflective Workbook for Parents and Families of Transgender and Non-Binary Children: Your Transition as Your Child Transitions by D. M. Maynard (Jessica Kingsley Publishers, 2020)

Helping your Transgender Teen by Irwin Kreiger (Genderwise Press, 2011)

Who are You? by Brook Pessin Whedbee (Jessica Kingsley Publishers, 2016)

Before I Had the Words by Skylar Kergil (Skyhorse, 2017)

Nonbinary: Memoirs of Gender and Identity edited by Micah Rajunav and A. Scott Duane (Columbia University Press, 2019)

He, She, They by Schuylar Bailar (Hachette Go, 2023)

He's Always Been My Son: A Mother's Story about Raising Her Transgender Son by Janna Barkin (Jessica Kingsley Publishers, 2017)

You can find an extensive list of more books and media posted by Stand With Trans here:

https://docs.google.com/document/d/19Sxj3xPOmPmEpt6lzwSX_x6Mz3qYIT1tG7M3jM-Dz2E

PODCASTS

He's Always Been My Son, A Mother's Story
An interview with Janna Barkin on the "Reflective Conversations on Gender Transition: An Educational Interview Series with D. M. Maynard" video podcast. Lilia's Livestreams:

https://youtu.be/WrptjaC6vak

A Mother's Story about Raising Her Transgender Son

An interview with Janna Barkin on "The Rise Parenting" podcast.

https://podcasts.apple.com/us/podcast/15-a-mothers-story-about-raising-her-transgender-son/id1460483402?i=1000463484323

A Mother Son Story of the Ultimate Transition
An interview with Alex, 15, and his mom about experiencing transition on the "Kelly Corrigan Wonders" podcast.

www.kellycorrigan.com/kelly-corrigan-wonders/alex

Endnotes

Introduction

1 Barkin, J. (2017) *He's Always Been My Son: A Mother's Story about Raising Her Transgender Son*. London: Jessica Kingsley Publishers.
2 www.thespahrcenter.org
3 The Trevor Project (2022) Research Brief: Behaviors of Supportive Parents and Caregivers for LGBTQ Youth. www.thetrevorproject.org/wp-content/uploads/2022/05/May-Research-Brief-Supportive-Care giver-Behavior.pdf

Janna's Top 5 Tips for Grandparents

1 Human Rights Campaign (2012) *Growing Up LGBT in America*. https://assets2.hrc.org/files/assets/resources/Growing-Up-LGBT-in-Amer ica_Report.pdf

What Does That Mean?

1 Price, M.N., & Green, A.E. (2021) "Association of gender identity acceptance with fewer suicide attempts among transgender and nonbinary youth." *Transgender Health 8*, 1. https://doi.org/10.1089/trgh.2021.0079
2 Gender Spectrum (n.d.) *The Language of Gender*. Retrieved September 12, 2023. www.genderspectrum.org/home
3 www.ucsfbenioffchildrens.org/clinics/child-and-adolescent-gender-center
4 American Psychiatric Association (2013) *Diagnostic and Statistical Manual of Mental Disorders* (5th ed.; DSM–5). Arlington, VA: American Psychiatric Association.

5   American Psychiatric Association (2023) "Gender dysphoria diagnosis." www.psychiatry.org/psychiatrists/diversity/education/transgender-and-gender-nonconforming-patients/gender-dysphoria-diagnosis

Part 1

1   Facebook (2023) "Being your authentic self on Facebook." www.facebook.com/help/186614050293763
2   Wilson, B., Choi, S., Herman, J., Becker, T., & Conron, K. (2017) *Characteristics and Mental Health of Gender Nonconforming Adolescents in California*. Los Angeles, CA: The Williams Institute and UCLA Center for Health Policy Research. https://williamsinstitute.law.ucla.edu/wp-content/uploads/GNC-Youth-CA-Dec-2017.pdf
3   Wilson, B.D.M., & Meyer, I.H. (2022) *Nonbinary LGBTQ Adults in the United States*. Los Angeles, CA: Williams Institute. https://williamsinstitute.law.ucla.edu/publications/nonbinary-lgbtq-adults-us
4   Henig, R.M. (2023) "How science is helping US understand gender." *National Geographic Magazine*. www.nationalgeographic.com/magazine/article/how-science-helps-us-understand-gender-identity
5   Travers, R., Bauer, G., Pyne, J., Bardley, K., Gale, L., & Papdimitriou, M. (2012) *Impacts of Strong Parental Support for Trans Youth: A Report Prepared for Children's Aid Society of Toronto and Delisle Youth Services*. Trans PULSE. http://transpulseproject.ca/wp-content/uploads/2012/10/Impacts-of-Strong-Parental-Support-for-Trans-Youth-vFINAL.pdf
6   Pew Research Center (2013) "A survey of LGBT Americans." https://www.pewresearch.org/social-trends/2013/06/13/a-survey-of-lgbt-americans
7   Minkin, R., & Brown, A. (2021) "Rising shares of U.S. adults know someone who is transgender or goes by gender-neutral pronouns." *Pew Research Center*. www.pewresearch.org/short-reads/2021/07/27/rising-shares-of-u-s-adults-know-someone-who-is-transgender-or-goes-by-gender-neutral-pronouns
8   Pew Research Center (2016) "5. Vast majority of Americans know someone who is gay, fewer know someone who is transgender." www.pewresearch.org/religion/2016/09/28/5-vast-majority-of-americans-know-someone-who-is-gay-fewer-know-someone-who-is-transgender
9   The Trevor Project (2022) *2022 National Survey on LGBTQ Youth Mental Health*. www.thetrevorproject.org/survey-2022

Part 2

1 Herman, J., Flores, A., Gates, G., & Brown, T. (2022) *How Many Adults and Youth Identify as Transgender in the United States?* Los Angeles, CA: Williams Institute. https://williamsinstitute.law.ucla.edu/publications/trans-adults-united-states

2 Brown, A. (2022) "About 5% of young adults in the U.S. say their gender is different from their sex assigned at birth." *Pew Research Center.* www.pewresearch.org/short-reads/2022/06/07/about-5-of-young-adults-in-the-u-s-say-their-gender-is-different-from-their-sex-assigned-at-birth

3 Herthel, J., Jennings, J., & McNicholas, S. (2014) *I Am Jazz.* New York: Dial Books.

Part 3

1 Simons, L., Schrager, S.M., Clark, L.F., Belzer, M., & Olson, J. (2013) "Parental support and mental health among transgender adolescents." *Journal of Adolescent Health 53*, 6, 791–793.

2 Crenshaw, K.W. (2017) "Demarginalizing the Intersection of Race and Sex: A Black Feminist Critique of Antidiscrimination Doctrine, Feminist Theory and Antiracist Politics." *University of Chicago Legal Forum 1989*, Article 8. https://chicagounbound.uchicago.edu/uclf/vol1989/iss1/8

3 McClurg, L. (2023) "Transgender and nonbinary people are up to six times more likely to have autism." *NPR.* www.npr.org/2023/01/15/1149318664/transgender-and-non-binary-people-are-up-to-six-times-more-likely-to-have-autism

4 Tannehill, B. (2018) *Everything You Ever Wanted to Know about Trans (But Were Afraid to Ask).* London: Jessica Kingsley Publishers.

5 The Trevor Project (2022) *Homelessness and Housing Instability Among LGBTQ Youth.* www.thetrevorproject.org/research-briefs/homelessness-and-housing-instability-among-lgbtq-youth-feb-2022

6 Patrick is happy with us referring to him as "Zoey" when talking about his early childhood here, for clarity's sake. It is worth noting again that many trans people would not want to be spoken about using previous names and pronouns, as discussed under "dead name" in the glossary.

Part 4

1 American Academy of Pediatrics (2022) *Promoting Healthy Development of Sexuality and Gender Identity.* Bright Futures. https://downloads.aap.org/AAP/PDF/BF_HealthySexualityGenderIdentity_Tipsheet.pdf

2   Parks, C., Guskin, E., & Clement, S. (2023) "Nov. 10-Dec. 1, 2022, Washington Post-KFF Trans in America Survey." *Washington Post*. www.washingtonpost.com/tablet/2023/03/23/nov-10-dec-1-2022-washington-post-kff-trans-survey

3   www.coastpride.org

4   Parks, C., Guskin, E., & Clement, S. (2023) "Nov. 10-Dec. 1, 2022, Washington Post-KFF Trans in America Survey." *Washington Post*. www.washingtonpost.com/tablet/2023/03/23/nov-10-dec-1-2022-washington-post-kff-trans-survey

Part 5

1   Travers, R., Bauer, G., Pyne, J., Bardley, K., Gale, L., & Papdimitriou, M. (2012) *Impacts of Strong Parental Support for Trans Youth: A Report Prepared for Children's Aid Society of Toronto and Delisle Youth Services*. Trans PULSE. http://transpulseproject.ca/wp-content/uploads/2012/10/Impacts-of-Strong-Parental-Support-for-Trans-Youth-vFINAL.pdf

2   The Trevor Project (2019) "The Trevor Project research brief: Accepting adults reduce suicide attempts among LGBTQ youth." www.thetrevorproject.org/wp-content/uploads/2019/06/Trevor-Project-Accepting-Adult-Research-Brief_June-2019.pdf

3   Kergil, S. (2017) *Before I Had the Words: On Being a Transgender Young Adult*. New York: Skyhorse.

4   Kergil, S. (n.d.). *skylarkeleven - YouTube*. www.youtube.com/user/skylarkeleven

5   Merriam-Webster Dictionary, "Accepting." https://www.merriam-webster.com/dictionary/accepting (accessed February 20, 2024).

6   Family Acceptance Project (2023) *Box*. San Francisco State University. https://sfsu.app.box.com/s/odbe5bz2p6nv7nh1el40e4viwgfrf7m4/file/1224834290658

7   Ryan, C., Russell, S.T., Huebner, D., Diaz, R., & Sanchez, J. (2010) "Family acceptance in adolescence and the health of LGBT young adults." *Journal of Child and Adolescent Psychiatric Nursing* 23, 4, 205–213.

8   Movement Advancement Project (2019) *Talking about Family Acceptance & Transgender Youth*. www.lgbtmap.org/file/talking-about-family-acceptance-transgender-youth.pdf

9   Family Acceptance Project (2023) *Box*. San Francisco State University. https://sfsu.app.box.com/s/odbe5bz2p6nv7nh1el40e4viwgfrf7m4/file/1224834290658

10 Andrzejewski, J., Pampati, S., Steiner, R.J., Boyce, L., & Johns, M.M. (2020) "Perspectives of transgender youth on parental support: Qualitative findings from the resilience and transgender youth study." *Health Education & Behavior 48*, 1, 74–81.

Part 6

1 UCSF Center of Excellence for Transgender Health https://transcare. ucsf.edu

UCSF Child and Adolescent Gender Center: www. ucsfbenioffchildrens.org/clinics/child-and-adolescent-gender-center

Mount Sinai Center for Transgender Medicine and Surgery: www. mountsinai.org/locations/center-transgender-medicine-surgery

Children's Hospital Los Angeles: www.chla.org/adolescent-and-young-adult-medicine/center-transyouth-health-and-development

2 Boston Children's Hospital (n.d.) Gender Multispecialty Service (GeMS). www.childrenshospital.org/programs/gender-multispecialty-service

3 Kost, R. (2017) "Finding himself: Transgender child, parents sort through new reality." *San Francisco Chronicle*, June 18. https://proj ects.sfchronicle.com/2017/transgender-child

Part 8

1 Travers, R., Bauer, G., Pyne, J., Bardley, K., Gale, L., & Papdimitriou, M. (2012) *Impacts of Strong Parental Support for Trans Youth: A Report Prepared for Children's Aid Society of Toronto and Delisle Youth Services*. Trans PULSE. http://transpulseproject.ca/wp-content/uploads/2012/10/Impacts-of-Strong-Parental-Support-for-Trans-Youth-vFINAL.pdf

2 On June 12, 2016, a gunman opened fire at Pulse, a gay nightclub in Orlando, Florida. Fifty people were killed and another 58 were injured in what was noted as the deadliest mass shooting in recent history in the United States.

3 Scott-Hainchek, S. (2018). "Oxford English Dictionary: Singular "they" is totally OK." *The Fussy Librarian, October 1*. www.thefussylibrarian. com/newswire/for-authors/2018/10/01/oxford-english-dictionary-singular-they-is-totally-ok

Thank You

First and foremost, this book could not have come to be without the love and support of my husband Gabriel. With his excellent editing skills, he crafted my pieces and stories into a cohesive manuscript ready for the publishers. Thank you dear Gabriel; my love, my life partner, my rock.

Special thanks to all the wonderful folks at Jessica Kingsley Publishers for their time, attention, and enthusiasm in bringing this project to fruition.

A note of gratitude to my accountability buddy Lesley Smith. Our meetings kept me on track and encouraged me to get to the finish line.

Big thanks to my mental health team who helped me through the rough patches along the way.

Thank you to my son Amaya for allowing me to share what is essentially his story so publicly. He is the reason I started this work, and his encouragement to keep going is vital. He once said to me, "I don't know where I would be without you." I told him, "That's exactly the point of what I do and why I do it."

Finally, thank you to the dear grandparents and grandchildren who contributed to *A Grand Love*. This book could not have happened without your stories. I am deeply moved by your narratives

and so grateful to you for sharing your experiences a.
with us. It is my hope that sharing these stories will foste.
compassion, understanding, and acceptance in society.